How to Read the Victorian Novel

How to Study Literature

The books in this series – all written by eminent scholars renowned for their teaching abilities – show students how to read, understand, write, and criticize literature. They provide the key skills which every student of literature must master, as well as offering a comprehensive introduction to the field itself.

Published

How to Read the Victorian Novel

George Levine

Blackwell
Publishing

BLACKWELL PUBLISHING
350 Main Street, Malden, MA 02148–5020, USA
9600 Garsington Road, Oxford OX4 2DQ, UK
550 Swanston Street, Carlton, Victoria 3053, Australia

The right of George Levine to be identified as the author of this work has been asserted in accordance with the UK Copyright, Designs, and Patents Act 1988.

Designations used by companies to distinguish their products are often claimed as trademarks. All brand names and product names used in this book are trade names, service marks, trademarks, or registered trademarks of their respective owners. The publisher is not associated with any product or vendor mentioned in this book.

This publication is designed to provide accurate and authoritative information in regard to the subject matter covered. It is sold on the understanding that the publisher is not engaged in rendering professional services. If professional advice or other expert assistance is required, the services of a competent professional should be sought.

First published 2008 by Blackwell Publishing Ltd

1   2008

Library of Congress Cataloging-in-Publication Data

Levine, George Lewis.
    How to read the Victorian novel / by George Levine.
        p. cm.—(How to study literature)
    Includes bibliographical references (p.) and index.
    ISBN 978-1-4051-3055-4 (hardcover : alk. paper)—ISBN 978-1-4051-3056-1 (pbk. : alk. paper)   1. English fiction—19th century—History and criticism.   2. English fiction—19th century—Examinations—Study guides.   3. Literature and society—England—History—19th century.   4. Books and reading—Social aspects—England—History—19th century.   5. Senses and sensation in literature.   6. Bildungsromans, English—History and criticism.   I. Title.
    PR871.L48 2008
    823'.809—dc22

                                                                      2007013152

A catalogue record for this title is available from the British Library.

Set in 10.5/13pt Minion
by Graphicraft Limited, Hong Kong
Printed and bound in Singapore
by Utopia Press Pte Ltd

The publisher's policy is to use permanent paper from mills that operate a sustainable forestry policy, and which has been manufactured from pulp processed using acid-free and elementary chlorine-free practices. Furthermore, the publisher ensures that the text paper and cover board used have met acceptable environmental accreditation standards.

For further information on
Blackwell Publishing, visit our website at
www.blackwellpublishing.com

Contents

Preface

The reign of Queen Victoria ran from 1837 to 1901. In 1837 Charles Dickens was publishing *Oliver Twist*. In 1901 Rudyard Kipling published *Kim*. These books are worlds apart, geographically, chronologically, but not entirely technically. Between those two books, thousands of "Victorian novels" were published, and their differences are often as wide as the difference between Dickens and Kipling, sometimes wider. The narrative similarities in the treatment of the two young protagonists, wandering loose in a difficult world, given the geographical and cultural differences, is quite striking. The assumption of this study is that it is worth thinking about how or whether the rubric "Victorian novel" can apply to them. We think of a "Victorian novel" as a familiar and comfortable – sometimes boring or prudish – sort of book, even when we haven't read it. The object of this study is, first, to try to figure out what makes books so diverse as these "Victorian novels," and then to demonstrate that they are less familiar than they seem, more historically conditioned, and distinctly less comfortable, quaint, cute, and predictable than BBC and film productions have made many people think they are.

To accomplish this, it's necessary to start at the beginning, recognizing that the number and variety of Victorian novels makes any introduction to the field inevitably selective. An absolutely comprehensive consideration of "how to read the Victorian novel" would, among other things, require extensive chapters on books like *Kim*, which move out of England's green and pleasant land and the world of domestic fiction into the empire, and like the early works of Conrad, who is most often regarded as a "modernist," though even *Lord Jim* (1900) is, strictly speaking, Victorian. It would, moreover, require a chapter on children's fiction, like Charles Kingsley's

Water Babies (1863), or John Ruskin's *King of the Golden River* (1851), and, particularly, Lewis Carroll's Alice stories (1865; 1871). There are plenty of gothic fictions mixed in to Victoriana, and a chapter on *Dracula* and its scary kin would be in order. So too would a chapter on adventure fiction like that of Frederick Marryat (which very few people, relatively speaking, read any longer). Or how about, one might legitimately ask, Utopian (or anti-Utopian) fiction like William Morris's *News from Nowhere* (1890), or Samuel Butler's *Erewhon* (1872)?

In view of this enormous, sublimely mountainous heap of possible books and kinds of books, I have decided that this study should concentrate its attention on the most familiar and impressive achievements of Victorian fiction in order to locate fundamental elements that allow us to character-ize novels as Victorian with more than chronological significance, *and* in order to intimate possibilities that extend well beyond them. This book should be understood as an opening onto the vast panorama of Victorian fiction, not a comprehensive reading and classification of it. But that opening is intended to defamiliarize what is conventionally thought of as familiar, to suggest that the Victorian novel is not so easy, so craftless, so mild, so tame and comfortable as it is conventionally taken to be.

One of the dominant assumptions under which I have worked might be taken, in the context of contemporary criticism, as conservative. It is that these classic texts, *Vanity Fair, Bleak House, David Copperfield, Jane Eyre, Middlemarch*, among others, very much deserve their standing as among the most interesting and important, and that they are by far the most useful for helping us understand not only what the dominant concerns, aesthetic, moral, and epistemological, of the Victorians were, but what sorts of cul-tural assumptions underlay the art and craft of Victorian fiction writing. The implicit argument throughout the book is that these are resistant works as much as they are acquiescent ones. That is, in their uniqueness, in the intensity and craft with which they investigate the lives and minds of their protagonists and the circumstances out of which they come, they are not merely constructions confirming, as much contemporary criticism has it, the status quo, the moral and social conventions that the new bourgeoisie was developing. They were not merely models of non-rebellious behavior and instruction manuals for those living in or entering the newly middle-class society in a capitalist economy. As much as they are books of their time, they were also books written partly against the grain of their cul-tures. They are not comfortable, or should not be read as such. They are exploratory and inquisitive as well as didactic and moralistic.

One major problem with a book of this size with these large ambitions is that many of the concerns of the most recent criticism of Victorian fiction could not be addressed at length – concerns about gender, about empire, about the sheer materiality of Victorian culture, for example. But in attempting to think about what kind of equipment one needs for "reading" Victorian fiction, I came to believe that one needs first a command of the mainstream. I don't for an instant want this book to intimate that there isn't a lot more where this came from, that Mrs. Oliphant, for example, is not worth a great deal more than I have been able to say about her here, or that George Meredith shouldn't have been attended to, or that Trollope shouldn't have been featured as prominently as these other great writers, or that the great army of interesting women novelists shouldn't have been represented. In preparation for this study, I read, among others, several novels of Dinah Mulock Craik, I read *Robert Elsmere* (1888), I reread Anne Brontë's novels. There was a world of fiction waiting to be mentioned. I don't mean to ignore the extraordinary moral complications that came with the development of the new bourgeois culture into which these books were written, or to forget how many of the books are implicitly though not explicitly dependent on the economic conditions of the empire.

But it became clear to me that the best way in was through those familiar texts, whose presence in English speaking culture has obviously marked that culture, and whose very familiarity helps in the work of "defamiliarizing," which I believe is critically important if readers are to feel the full strength of these works and of other Victorian novels waiting there in the wings. Recognizing what it is that is fundamental to these works, and how they explore and criticize the new Victorian world they are trying to describe and create, makes it a lot easier to move on later to fuller cultural critiques, both of the novel and of the culture.

My strategy has been to open with a long survey-like chapter, aimed at trying to locate those qualities that most consistently mark Victorian fiction, of whatever type, recognizing that no single book is likely to manifest all of these qualities. In concentrating on certain key ethical and epistemological questions as they effect the shape of the genre, the imagination of character, the direction of narratives, the first chapter is intended to open the way for all that follows. The following chapters expand on the key elements described in the first chapter.

It did not seem to me fruitful, as I originally intended, to offer a set of nuanced readings of classic Victorian novels. To think about "how to read" the Victorian novel one doesn't need to have thrust upon one someone else's reading. The four central chapters are designed not around particular books but around dominant elements in and problems raised by Victorian fiction. And it seemed best to work out that thematic organization by keeping always in mind, for each subject, a particular text to which I could make regular reference as example. Thus, when talking about the beginnings of the Victorian novel and its relation to publication practices, I focused on *Pickwick Papers*, for obvious reasons, without any attempt to "read" the book thoroughly.

Chapter three engages realism, the dominant literary mode of the period. No study of the Victorian novel can get far without coming to terms, in some way or other, with "realism," but the Victorian version is something quite different from, say, continental realism. And while, as I've already suggested alluding to a whole range of other books, realism was not the exclusive mode of Victorian fiction, it was the most characteristic, and infected even those forms that seemed not to be realistic at all. So this book locates the most characteristically Victorian quality of the novel in the special kind of realism that writers like Thackeray (in his way) and George Eliot (in hers) practiced. To follow the fate of the Victorian novel is to follow the fate of realism with all its complex epistemological and ethical twists and turns.

The two key chapters that follow take up two large subgenres of the Victorian novel, the *Bildungsroman* and the sensation novel. There is obviously something quite arbitrary about this, but the rationale is not arbitrary. I take the fundamental tradition of the novel to be intimately connected to the tradition of the *Bildungsroman*. If one considers *Don Quixote* to be one of the key texts in the developing history of the novel, one can see that the *Bildungsroman* will be an almost inevitable development. The Don misreads books of fantasy as Maggie Tulliver misreads a whole series of texts, including *The Imitation of Christ*, and her actions and mistakes are shaped in great part by that reading. That, in one form at least, is the *Bildung* story, although of course, the *Bildung* protagonist will – in most cases – get a chance to grow out of the delusions into a more practical engagement with "reality." Realism and *Bildung* flow into each other, and a large proportion of Victorian realist fiction is entirely, or in part, *Bildung* fiction as well.

The sensation novel as the next of the chapters would seem a more arbitrary choice. But the point of choosing that decade-long extravaganza of scandal and mistaken identity (for the sensation novel fizzled out rather quickly after the 1860s) is that it gives an opportunity for two things – first, to demonstrate how beneath the domestic surface of realist fiction there are all sorts of violent and scandalous things going on, or trying to. Sensation fiction helps problematize the tradition of realist fiction. Second, the consideration of the sensation novel works as part of a demonstration of the arbitrariness of categories, suggesting that "the Victorian novel" exists not as a neatly definable category but rather on a long continuum. With a little shift of emphasis, a sensation novel becomes a *Bildungsroman,* or vice versa – the example of *Great Expectations* is a perfect one here. The *Bildungsroman* and the sensation novel turn out to be more than kissing cousins; realism in its Victorian version, domestic, compromising, turns out to have elements in it that resist the very compromises it affirms. As the first chapter argues, there is a set of (varying) family connections that make the most diverse sorts of books clearly Victorian. Looking at how the sensation novel works helps, perhaps more than the study of a more obviously representative novel, to make those connections evident.

The last chapter *is* a study of a particular novel, perhaps the most representative of all Victorian novels (if it makes sense to talk of anything being *most* representative), *Middlemarch*. But it is not offered as a reading. Rather, the book becomes a locus that allows readers to see the general ideas offered earlier embodied and working in an important text. So the very long study of *Middlemarch* might be read as the first chapter revisited, but this time with an emphasis on how the various elements that create family resemblance among Victorian novels actually work in a particular text. Seeing these elements at work and juxtaposed re-enforces the sense of continuity, of family resemblance, of something distinctly Victorian, at the same time as it reveals how so many of these common elements work resistantly, and how, when fully developed, they lead in directions beyond the Victorian novel itself, calling its very practices into question.

But, in the end, all one can do in a book of this sort is point. There is the center of the Victorian achievement. There is what lies outside the center but needs attention. It is an enormous canon of works. The Victorian novel represents one of the great achievements of English literature. I hope that, with all its conscious and unconscious limitations, this study might serve as at least a small opening into so vast and wonderful a world.

Chapter 1

What's Victorian about the Victorian Novel?

It's hard to say what the "Victorian novel" is, no less "how to read it." The best definition is not very useful, but is at least literally correct. That is, "Victorian novel," in the most literal and precise sense, means any novel written in England between, roughly, 1837 and 1901, the dates of Queen Victoria's reign. That obviously doesn't get us very far. It leaves the question of whether "Victorian novel" is anything but a chronological classification. What could there possibly be in common among writers as various as Dickens, whose first books actually predated Victoria's coronation, the Brontë sisters, Thackeray, Disraeli, Marryat, Gaskell, Charles Lever and Charles Reade, Margaret Oliphant and Dinah Mulock Craik, George Eliot, Charles Kingsley, Anthony Trollope, and his mother, Frances Trollope, and Bulwer Lytton, Joseph Conrad, Wilkie Collins, Mary Elizabeth Braddon, Thomas Hardy, George Meredith, Charlotte Yonge, Marie Corelli, Mrs. Humphrey Ward, George Gissing, and George Moore? Of course, there are dozens of other "Victorian novelists," but this list should suffice to make clear that "Victorian novel" is an all-inclusive and therefore crude category, at best. It contains all kinds of subspecies or subgenres, most of them actually crossing categories, and all themselves difficult to categorize simply – romance, sensation novel, industrial novel, *Bildungsroman*, fantasy, historical novel, multiplot novel, autobiographical novel, adventure novel, realist novel.

And yet, despite the enormous diversity, it makes some sense still to try to think about "the Victorian novel" as a distinctive kind of novel, to whatever subgenre any of its members might belong. It makes sense to try to get at qualities that might be considered distinctive of the Victorian novel, and consider that there might be common ways to read it. It is not that there are uniquely "Victorian" characteristics that, once identified, would be recognized as diagnostic, and as revelatory clues to how the books should be read, and it is certainly not that all such characteristics emerge in all of the novels called "Victorian." Dickens simply does not write the way George Eliot wrote, nor about the same things, nor from the same perspective. His novels are structured differently; his prose is more flamboyant and spectacular; he is yet more attuned to surfaces and given to big moments and narrative extravagance and metaphorical excess. It is of no little significance that Dickens's novels were almost all published in parts, over long stretches of time, and before he had completed the whole book. Notoriously, he usually wrote to the edge of each monthly deadline. On the other hand, George Eliot abjured extravagance, in prose or situation, and insisted (sometimes not altogether consistently with the way her novels play out) on the importance of the ordinary; she writes an analytic and precisely intellectual prose, with greater attention to interiority than to material surfaces, and builds her drama largely from psychological exploration – though always within historically located moments. Her concern for the art of her work made parts publication (before the whole was completed) anathema to her, while at the same time she did publish several of her novels in parts. Yet these two utterly distinctive writers are also distinctly "Victorian novelists." To borrow a line from *Bleak House*: "what connection can there be?"

That question, in a way, is the dominant subject of this book. Is there something that makes a novel "Victorian" besides the date of its publication? Are there any distinguishing Victorian traits that can help us maneuver through the novels of *both* Dickens and George Eliot? Of *both* Wilkie Collins and Elizabeth Gaskell? Of *both* Thackeray and Hardy? One might reasonably ask, then, what makes the Victorian novel *Victorian*. Getting a feel for the diversity and diffusiveness of Victorian narratives, the remarkable variety of styles and forms these books adopt, the range of characters they include, the importantly different understandings of questions we might solemnly call epistemological and ethical, will help toward a recognition that after all, across all the variety, the Victorian novel is a subject in itself, and a subject worth pursuing.

Putting aside the obvious evidence of chronology, we are likely to sense the Victorianness of Victorian novels just because they return so often to certain themes and subjects, position themselves morally in relation to those subjects and themes, develop ways of perceiving and narrating that, however much they differ in detail, simply feel Victorian. It is not that, as we read, we consciously and rationally tote up the recurrences: for example, the almost romantic insistence that the subject is *not* romantic, the deliberate assertions of ordinariness, the preoccupation with childhood and innocence and misguided romantic ambition, the overriding emphasis on domestic dramas and the insular feel even as on the margins the empire looms large, the pervasive sensitivity to class and the struggles over class positions, the almost dominant importance of money, negatively or positively, in the moral plotting of the stories, the flights of sentimentality, the delicious lingering over pathetic deaths, the omniscient narrator's modes and intrusions and moral commentary, the focus on details of domestic life, the providential plot worked out without more than token reference to providential control, the "angel in the house" representation of women, the multi-plottedness and diversity of focus, the sense that all things, however disguised the connections might be, are organically connected, the *Bildung* narrative. And this list might be extended considerably.

But no single quality of this sort, and no formal tabulation of accumulations of such qualities, will settle identification. These qualities exist in relation to the Victorian novel as a whole rather as family resemblances relate to any given family – as Wittgenstein developed the point. "Family resemblances," though we notice them almost intuitively, are pretty decisive, both for our identification of novels and for much of the ordinary business of our lives. We have a sense of the meaning of words without being able to list in detail all the possible meanings or provide a thorough definition. Family resemblances don't wait upon analytic proof; they depend (as do so many Victorian novels) on the rather mixed and imperfect nature of most ostensibly absolute classifications. Although members of any family are likely to resemble each other, each member looks recognizably different. We might recognize, say, a family chin, or the family eyes, but no member of the family is likely to have *all* of the family traits, the eyes, the chin, the high cheekbones, the blonde hair; and no single trait is likely to be present in *all* the family members. Victorian novels, like such a family, are all distinctly different and yet all have enough traits in common to make them recognizably "Victorian."

The more Victorian novels we know, the more confidently intuitive we can be about those family resemblances. If, say, *Bleak House* (1852) is a novel deeply concerned with the whole range of Victorian society and with the problem of connections from event to event, from person to person, from class to class, and *Jane Eyre* (1847) is restricted in its range of reference and seems not to want to move beyond the enclosed story of Jane, in her relations to St. John and, primarily, to Rochester, the two novels are nevertheless much more closely related thematically and technically than either of them is, say, to a modernist novel like James Joyce's *The Portrait of the Artist as a Young Man* (1916), even though that novel has much in it that does recall the concerns of the Victorians. The chronological difference suggests a thematic and technical distance, a broad cultural difference, recognition of which can intensify our awareness of the family resemblances that connect Victorian novels.

Joyce's Stephen Daedalus sets out in the last pages to "forge in the smithy of my soul, the uncreated conscience of my race." In one sense that heroic sounding and enormously ambitious insistence is closely connected to the noble or romantic aspirations of young Victorian *Bildung*'s heroes, but nobody has ever mistaken Joyce's novels for Victorian, or Stephen Daedalus for a Victorian character. The distance between him and a Victorian novelist protagonist, like Arthur Pendennis of Thackeray's *Pendennis* (1850), is enormous. Penn begins as a romantic, proceeds through a series of disillusionments, and ends in a compromise between what conventional romance requires and what he can any longer believe. He has no illusions about forging in the smithy of his soul anything at all. Stephen, perhaps in his way also "romantic," is ambitious and idealistic even at the end, where in a Victorian *Bildung* of that sort, the protagonist would be reduced, as Penn is, to a long series of what Penn calls "buts," that is, reservations about what is possible, about what he can do. Penn's vocation is hardly "art" in a modernist sense. He is in the commerce of novel-writing. Yet in the manner of the *Bildungsroman* the figures are similarly traced from childhood to the edge of maturity, as is David Copperfield, another successful novelist at the end, and Jane Eyre herself, who has no artistic pretensions. Although *Jane Eyre* is a *Bildungsroman* (though distinctly a woman's), its protagonist aspires to a freedom that has no Daedaelian element at all. And *Bleak House*, at least in the Esther sections, has its own *Bildung* patterns, but no figure in it with such aspirations – for both protagonists something like domestic tranquility is the aim and the result.

The differences within similarities extend, for *The Portrait of the Artist as a Young Man* does not encourage a sense of cozy familiarity that many readers think they find in Victorian novels, and that, despite some extremes of plotting (including in *Bleak House* a murder mystery and in *Jane Eyre* the violence of Bertha, Rochester's first wife). Joyce's work is overtly experimental in form even as it replays the *Bildungsroman* (or *Künstleroman*) conventions. It does not offer itself as the kind of novel Penn or David might write, but as a strenuously brilliant manipulation of techniques and language that makes no compromise with the reader, no effort to appeal to existing tastes in the novel-reading public. Moreover, the quasi-heroic implication of exile is largely incompatible with the tendencies in Victorian fiction to regard exile as virtually the ultimate punishment, the expulsion from the community; in *Adam Bede* (1859), for example, it is the price that Hetty Sorrel and Arthur Donnithorne must pay for their sins. While there is in *The Portrait of the Artist* an echo of the plot of George Eliot's final novel, *Daniel Deronda* (1876), it is an *aesthetic* echo of an *ethical* ambition and is even more open-ended than *Daniel Deronda* itself, and it requires for its unfolding no girl/boy romance. But *Daniel Deronda* is itself something of an aberration, a last gasp of Victorianism by a writer who was by that time close to giving up on English culture.

Portrait is clearly and originally artful; its art gathers attention rather than deflects it and art is certainly its subject, even in its innovative rendering of consciousness. It has, on the other hand, long been a given of criticism of Victorian fiction that the Victorian novelists were not very artful, as Joyce always and certainly is.[1] David Copperfield, like Stephen Daedalus, is an artist, and the central consciousness of a *Bildungsroman*, yet David's narrative, although I would argue that it is as experimentally fresh and brilliant as Stephen's, is rarely treated by critics as an artistic innovation however much it is respected and its virtuosity recognized. *David Copperfield* (1850) feels comfortably familiar and is never difficult to read. Instead of the powerful aesthetic thrust, both embodied and thematized in Joyce, there is a powerful moral thrust and the art that enters as subject is assimilated to an ethic of hard work leading to worldly profit. It would hardly be appropriate to talk of the coziness of Joyce's fictional world, which constantly drives us out of any complacent sense of psychology, ethics, or literature, and refuses that warm and helpful connection with the reader that one finds in *David Copperfield* and many other Victorian novels. Against the rigors of modernism and its aesthetic austerity, there appears to be something comfortingly familiar in Dickens' strategies of representation.

It is not hard, then, to feel the difference between "modernist" and "Victorian" fiction. But for a long time, it was implicitly or explicitly assumed that the difference was also a matter of quality. Joyce's rigorous artfulness might have been taken as one landmark of the qualitative difference. The Victorians, the assumption went, simply were aesthetically naïve. The implicit judgment of aesthetic weakness, which has in recent decades significantly diminished, was built upon what ought to be recognized as our own historically constrained sense of art.[2] Modernist art had to define itself by rejecting its immediate predecessors, and the Victorians were the hated parents, rather as the transition is implicitly represented in Samuel Butler's *The Way of All Flesh* (1903), in which the young Ernest Pontifex can only make his way in the world by being cut loose from his very Victorian parents, and in a novel where Victorian ways are uproariously and painfully represented and satirized. In such a book, as in the literary movements that opened the way to Lawrence, Woolf, Joyce, and T. S. Eliot, it would have been impossible and counterproductive to look at the parents and their culture with the sort of psychological penetration and sympathetic engagement that, for example, George Eliot's realism would have required.

Our contemporary conventions of reading, then, are partly shaped by the particular history of our culture's response to the "classics" of Victorian fiction. Outside of the rebellious world of high modernist art, Victorian fiction has almost always produced a sense of comforting familiarity, deriving from the narrators' overt concern in addressing the reader, but allied as well to a nostalgic aura that hangs over many of the novels, which reflect a culture more than 100 years dead, and tend themselves to look back a generation or two for their subjects. The Victorian novel built on the tradition that Walter Scott had largely created on his own, beginning with *Waverley, or 'tis Sixty Years Since* (1814), the tradition of looking back two generations to a historical moment now passed but deeply interesting and formative of contemporary life. Scott-like nostalgia has been much encouraged by the costume-drama quality of most television and film recreations of Victorian fiction. Coming to the novels now, it is hard not to assume that they are "easy," in comparison, certainly, with the works of high modernism, like Joyce's. It feels easy to maneuver through them, to predict the directions of their narratives, to gather the "morals" that seem to underlie their stories, and to follow the lines of the plot without much worry about implications unstated, artful devices neatly disguised, or literary relations. Much of the pleasure of re-engaging with Victorian novels comes from that sense of familiarity they produce, along with their quaint, often pre-industrial settings. (On the other hand, the subgenre of the "industrial novel," so very much in the center of contro-versial developments in the nineteenth century, and preoccupied with factories and grit and poverty and what was then the new world of Vict-orian industrialism, ironically also creates now a sense of familiarity, for these novels are particularly good as costume drama, as well. Moreover, the moralizing of the narrative and the efforts toward comic resolution seem to make more acceptable much of the grit, although continental novels, like Zola's *Germinal*, simply don't.)

Against this cozy sense of the Victorian novel that suggests its trans-parent readability, there is the characteristically modern, less sentimentally indulgent response that was until the 1960s probably the dominant response of critics and artists. It might be neatly, if only partially, repres-ented by Virginia Woolf's comment on George Eliot. Praising *Middlemarch* (1872), she famously called it "one of the few English novels written for grown-up people."[3] This sounds very favorable, and yet it also implies a strong negative judgment. Where does the comment on the rarity of *Middlemarch*'s virtues leave us in relation to novels like *Bleak House* or *Vanity Fair* (1848) or *The Last Chronicle of Barset* (1867)? Are these all childish?

Modernist artists, anticipated by Butler, looked away from their Vict-orian fathers, denigrating Victorian fiction because of its provincialism, its moralizing of experience, its tendencies to sentimentality and melodrama, its evasiveness about sexuality, its aesthetic simplicity, and its fairy-tale vision of things. Held up against the great nineteenth-century novelists of France and Russia, the Victorians were seen as almost childish. Even more recently, in one of the most important and distinguished books about the nineteenth-century novel, Franco Moretti has talked about the "judi-cial fairy-tale model"[4] that dominates the English novel, and particularly that very popular form of it that focuses on the development of young protagonists (the *Bildungsroman*).

In the last half of the twentieth century, when modernism itself was being displaced by new perspectives and when the resentment against Victorian patriarchs (and matriarchs) had subsided, Victorian fiction has been extensively reconsidered and re-evaluated. It has become clear that modernist judgments are not adequate to the achievement or to the matur-ity of the great Victorian fiction. Certainly, many of the classic Victorian novels make delightful reads for anyone at whatever level of sophistication about Victorian literature and culture, but Victorian fiction deserves to be recognized as one of the great achievements in the long history of English literature. To come to terms with the richness and complexity of Victorian narrative art, it will be important not to relax into the coziness that their familiarity now tends to produce, to recognize not only their aesthetic and cultural sophistication, but to feel the strength of their difficulties and resistances, and to understand their strangeness as well. For while these novels have been deeply influential within English speaking culture, they are indeed "strange." They develop from and speak to historically different cultures. The nostalgic indulgence with which modern readers tend to regard these novels does no justice either to their historical particularity, or to their importance in helping to create Victorian culture, in finding innovative ways to think about individuals and their psychology, in coming to terms with new urban societies, in defining and resisting the new bourgeois culture and the new capitalist economy, in reconciling traditional religious culture with the new forces for secularity, in managing all this with a new aesthetic seriousness and aesthetic experimentation. These are strange and powerful books we are dealing with: they have shaped some of the dominant myths of our culture. And at times, if we look back to them with fresh eyes, we find that however conventional they may at first seem, they are raising dangerously disruptive questions.

The point is not to make something difficult out of an art that has been seen as too easy. But it is to make something yet more interesting out of things already interesting, in part by intensifying our awareness of difference. The work is not to demystify our confident assumptions, as much contemporary criticism tries to do, but to remystify. That is, this book is designed in part to jar us loose from some of that sense of familiarity and coziness that has seemed to accompany our contemporary experience of Victorian fiction. If, in its apparent simplicity, its apparent indifference to the aesthetic rigors that were to become the very substance of early modernist art, the Victorian novel seems to the modern reader the most accessible and therefore the least disturbing of traditional literary works, that "seeming" is profoundly misleading. The arts of the Victorian novel suggest something else entirely – a literary form that participated in a developing revolution in reading habits and in self-understanding (and it is partly its success in these enterprises that makes the Victorian novel seem so familiar to modern readers). Understanding the kinds of preoccupations that drive the narratives of Victorian fiction requires acts of historical imagination. Understanding how the formal looseness and bagginess of so much Victorian fiction becomes a form of remarkable art requires acts of aesthetic imagination. Understanding the role of narrators or the peculiar focus of the literary traditions at work in the great Victorian novels requires acts of critical imagination. It is not enough to bring to bear on Victorian fiction the assumptions that govern our relations to modern fiction, the assumptions that drove the development of the novel from Henry James onward.

II

The Victorian novel emerges relatively early in the history of modern fiction, about a century on from the work of Defoe and Richardson and Fielding, and it took its shape when novel-reading was still far more a phenomenon of popular culture than of serious art (that distinction is, itself, a peculiarly nineteenth-century invention that emerged in part because the province of literature and the provenance of writers had so greatly expanded). The Victorian novel emerges from a condition perhaps most delightfully marked by Jane Austen's satiric defense of novels in *Northanger Abbey* (1818):

> There seems almost a general wish of decrying the capacity and undervaluing the labour of the novelists, and of slighting the performances which have only genius, wit, and taste to recommend them. "I am no novel reader – I seldom look into novels – Do not imagine that *I* often read novels – It is really very well for a novel." Such is the common cant. – "And what are you reading, Miss —?" "Oh, it is only a novel!" replies the young lady; while she lays down her book with affected indifference, or momentary shame. – "It is only *Cecilia*, or *Camilla*, or *Belinda*"; or, in short, only some work in which the greatest powers of the mind are displayed, in which the most thorough knowledge of human nature, the happiest delineation of its varieties, the liveliest effusions of wit and humour are conveyed to the world in the best chosen language.[5]

Austen's ironies suggest very clearly what was then the place of the novel in the English hierarchy of art, and it is important to note that while she understands respectable public opinion to be contemptuous of mere fiction, she has herself already come around to the view that the novel is one of the highest forms of art. In the course of the nineteenth century, Austen's judgment was to become the dominant one, but through a large part of the Victorian period, novels were still only partly integrated into the modern hierarchy of art, and a significant proportion of Victorian novels hardly deserve Austen's praise. But then, at any moment, only a small proportion of what is written is likely to achieve the ideals that Austen's narrator announces. When George Eliot was laying the ground for her own career as a serious novelist, she tried in her essay writing to clear the ground, discriminating between "silly novels by lady novelists" and the serious work that the novel might really do.[6]

Certainly, it was the case that many, probably most, Victorian novelists came from outside the cultured elite that had dominated "literature" well into the eighteenth century; many of the best-known Victorian novelists did not attend Oxbridge colleges and did not come from well established families. Many now famous writers became writers in large part as a way to make a living, and Anthony Trollope's comparison of the novelist to a shoemaker, however much it alarmed Henry James, was much more on the mark than many of us even now would like to admit. The nineteenth-century novel is full of reminders that writing novels was a business, and one that had serious effects not only on who could read those novels, but on how the novels were put together and what they were about.[7] Many of the most famous women writers of the period found in novel-writing a way to make a living rather than, at least to start with, a "vocation." Mrs. Oliphant, Mrs. Trollope, and Dinah Mulock Craik, among others, were staggeringly prolific writers, but their writing became both a means to survival and a force in the shaping of the novel as a form throughout the nineteenth century.

Doctor Johnson famously said that "No man but a blockhead ever wrote except for money," and the development of the Victorian novel almost fully confirms this view – no woman either. Although it would be wrong to assume that all Victorian novelists wrote strictly for money, it is clear that for every one the finances of novel-writing were a paramount condition for creativity. Writing had become a way to make a living, and for women in particular, with so narrow a range of possibilities for earning money and remaining respectable, novel-writing was a particularly satisfying vocation. The Grub Street that developed in the eighteenth century became the *New Grub Street* (1891) of George Gissing's novel, in which art and hackwork are seen as utterly antagonistic. The novel was a form that welcomed those not from traditionally wealthy and aristocratic families, and that gave impecunious women valuable economic opportunities. Certainly, the Victorian novel was the first major literary form that regularly gave prominence to women writers. When we think back now about who its greatest practitioners were, the names of George Eliot, Charlotte and Emily Brontë, and Elizabeth Gaskell are self-evidently prominent. The greatest writers were often also the best-paid ones.

Walter Scott, beginning in the second decade of the century, became the most influential writer in the history of the development of the novel, giving it an international popularity, extending its range, mixing domesticity with historical drama, giving a romantic aura to the details of ordinary life through the lens of history. Scott meant everything to the Victorians,[8] and one finds in rereading him that his influence on them included his attention to a dying past and to anthropologically fascinating lower-class figures and his mixing of historical reality with fictional plots and characters. His novels, which dramatize the tensions between old local cultures and civilizations and a new commercial, bourgeois middling society, are forced persistently to negotiate the transition, to determine a narrative relation to it; and in doing this, Scott's novels, which are notoriously about protagonists with divided loyalties, open up many of the problems that the Victorians would be facing.

Most famously, they have enormous difficulty imagining active and successful protagonists. One of the great ironies of these ostensibly romantic novels about world historical events is that "the hero of the Waverley novels"[9] – no matter how much he is dressed like the romantic hero – is usually weak, incapable of decisive action, morally divided, and much less interesting and attractive than the dark heroes, those like MacIvor in *Waverley*, or Regauntlet, who will stop at nothing to retain power and resist change, and who must die in the end. But Scott's protagonists might be considered tryouts for the male protagonists of Victorian novels, who tend to be weak, inefficacious, and psychologically divided as well.

Scott's financial troubles are legend, and his enormous productivity had a lot to do with his need to deal with his enormous debt. His very great popularity coincides with a vast expansion of the reading public, an expansion that in many ways affected the nature of the Victorian novel. No Victorian novelists could afford to ignore the publishing conditions that required "three-decker" novels, or novels written in weekly or monthly installments. And writers became popular because they wrote directly into the heart of the culture, directly into the developing world of bourgeois domestic life, where Scott's adventures were adored and countered by the kinds of compromises with the new civilization that Scott's books also ultimately claimed. Writing novels entailed engagement with the new audience, and the narrative stances of Victorian writers can often be traced back to this sense of a new audience with whom writers wanted to claim common cause.

The Victorian novel built itself partly on the ostensibly romantic thrills of Scottlike narratives, but most fundamentally on its preoccupation with domesticity, where the lives of women became central and where women, thus, gathered particular authority in the writing. Domestic realism spoke to the condition of its middle-class readers. The novel and the burgeoning middle class were, in Victorian England, deeply identified with each other, to the extent that many modern critics have viewed the Victorian novel as a kind of instruction book for the middle class.[10]

Yet committed as the Victorian novel is to representing this new reality and rejecting the literature of the past that now seemed irrelevant to this new life, it is not, any more than older forms, like epic and tragedy, outside of tradition and outside of *literary* traditions. Ironically, as I will try to show in future chapters, realism, the Victorian novel's primary method, whose determination to get at the truth entailed at least an overt rejection of merely literary forms, is thoroughly literary. It is so in two ways, primarily: first, it sets itself up as rejecting earlier literary representations and thus frequently re-enacts satirically aspects of more traditional literature. Satire is intrinsic to realism, and satire depends in part on knowledge of that earlier literature. So *Don Quixote*, a foundational text in the development of the European novel, which as everyone knows is an encyclopedic satire on romance, actually sustains a double relation to that earlier literature. On the one hand, it attributes the Don's madness to his reading too many romances and then failing to distinguish their fantasies from lived reality, and on the other, when the time comes to burn all the romance narratives that have led the Don astray, the Priest and the Barber linger lovingly over books they should be throwing into the pyre. Coming upon *Amadis of Gaul*, the Priest is ready to consign it to burning, but the Barber hesitates: "I . . . have heard say that this is the best of all the books of this kind ever written, and so, as something matchless in its own line, it ought to be pardoned."[11] More interesting and important yet is that the Priest and the Barber look at the title of every book and discuss its merits. Now I don't mean to suggest that exactly the same thing happens in Victorian realist fiction, but like *Don Quixote* Victorian realist fictions often turn on overreading protagonists and thus upon the reader knowing a past literature that is being either rejected or mimicked.

There is, however, another way in which realism is a very literary mode after all. That is, within the tradition (out of *Don Quixote*) of realism, it becomes difficult to distinguish realist conventions recognizable in the work of earlier writers from the effects of trying to describe the world as in itself it really is. It is not simply, for example, that many writers through their narrators will indicate other ways the story might have been told (invoking again literary forms that are being rejected), as Scott does it in *Waverley* or Thackeray very early on in *Vanity Fair*. It is that over and over again, novels will insist that the ordinary doings of its protagonists might reasonably be compared with the actions of epic heroes. Or that novel after novel will begin attempting to quiet expectations about great adventures and insisting, as Charlotte Brontë for example does at the start of *Shirley*: "If you think from this prelude that anything like a romance is preparing for you, reader, you never were more mistaken. Do you anticipate sentiment, and poetry, and reverie? Do you expect passion and stimulus, and melodrama? Calm your expectations: reduce them to a lowly standard." Passages with this kind of import abound in Victorian realist fiction, and even if they all perhaps arose spontaneously to the pens of so many different writers, it remains hard not to recognize this as a distinct *literary* convention. It in fact tells the reader a lot about how Victorian novelists imagine "realism." It should not take much of a reminder for us to realize that realism, say of the Zola or the Tolstoy schools, might assume very different relations to "stimulus" and "melodrama."

III

Despite, then, a certain anti-literary thrust, the Victorian novel, like all literature, tends to work within recognizable generic modes, and it is important to be able to recognize them and their traditions, and to recognize too how the enormous social and intellectual and imaginative energy that went into their production opened new forms, or developed old ones, and produced a remarkably fertile and rich thing called "the Victorian novel." The Victorian novel, for example, tends toward comic form, not of course in the sense that it is "funny," though very often it is very funny, but because as it pursues narratives of its largely middle-class protagonists, it tends to conclude in a movement toward union in marriage and in social harmony, with what we might call a "Pickwickian" affirmation of community and affection. Where, famously, and most particularly in the later parts of the century, it begins to resist that comic pattern, it fascinatingly develops new forms or evokes – as for instance Thomas Hardy often tried to do – classic patterns of tragedy.

Victorian fiction, however, rarely can be categorized simply and definitively. Tragedy and comedy coexist. A late novel like Hardy's *The Woodlanders* (1887) slips casually from tragedy to farce, from pastoral elegy to something like Restoration comedy, to symbolic and poetic lyric. It incorporates urban ennui and country bumpkin innocence. And if *The Woodlanders* is an extreme case of generic mix, it is not radically different, in that respect, from most of Dickens' novels, which shift from urban realism to melodrama and sentimentality. Even so moderate and consistent-toned a writer as Trollope fills his multiplotted novels with alternative treatments of similar motifs – as in *Can You Forgive Her* (1864), which in Alice, Glencora, and Mrs. Greenow plays out variations on common themes, almost farcical with Mrs. Greenow, approaching melodrama in Alice's story, and complexly realistic in Glencora's. The Victorian novel, on the whole, resists purity of form and rethinks narrative form in an expansive way that makes of it a fine instrument to register something of the social (religious and intellectual) transformations going on in the society all around it.

In addition, the Victorian novel often verges on the encyclopedic, so that while on the one hand we have a brilliant romance like *Wuthering Heights* (1847), compactly built around carefully managed and multiple perspectives, on the other we have the vast panorama of *Bleak House*, which quite explicitly from the start attempts to take as its dominant question, "What connection can there be?" What connection between the mud of London and the elegant grounds of a country aristocrat? Many of Dickens' novels take us through a wide range of class difference, and George Eliot's *Middlemarch* (1872), whose very middling name speaks much about the nature of Victorian fiction, in effect tries to represent a full (though provincial) community and in the context of a larger national history that fringes the personal narratives. One important – perhaps the most important and characteristic – mode of the Victorian novel is to stretch for eight hundred or so pages, embracing, it often feels, entire worlds and many different narrative lines. The effects of monthly publication, or of the "triple-decker" format for the lucrative lending library market, or of the installment format for weekly or monthly reviews – all of these are clearly visible in the texture of Victorian novels: their multiplicity of narrative lines, or the curious moments of suspense that punctuate them, or the leisurely dwelling on contextual details, or details of any sort, or the problems with overall architecture, or the tendency to imply a reader with whom the narrator seems to be in conversation.

Such multiplicities are implicated both in the very conditions of publication of these books and in the nature of the new society growing up around these novels, and reflected in them. Urban society, it is famously argued, puts in juxtaposition an enormous number of people who become more or less anonymous to each other. But the novelist's eye recognizes connections invisible to the participants, and the Victorian novel often becomes a kind of education in connectedness, with all the religious, ethical, and aesthetic implications the connectedness has. The Victorians inherited from their romantic predecessors (and contemporaries) an imagination of the organic connection among all things, connections natural, historical, religious, and ethical. "What connection can there be?" is a question that drives a significant proportion of Victorian novels as it drives the new social organizations that emerged from a culture of new anonymity and uncertainty of personal identity.

In dealing with these complications and multiplicities, this book then will attempt four closely related things: first, suggest the special nature of the context of the Victorian novel, in material terms (like that of publishing) and in cultural ones (concerning fundamental attitudes peculiar to the historical moment); second, make clear that the ostensibly casual form of most Victorian novels, which led Henry James to talk about a Trollope novel as a "loose, large, baggy monster," is not nearly as casual as it seems. Attention to the formal structures and strategies of the Victorian novel will allow a far stronger critical appreciation of the novels' achievements. Third, through a consideration of a series of classic Victorian narratives as they are related to major trends in fiction at the time, this book will try to register more fully the extraordinary diversity of Victorian novels while, at the same time, making some of those connections that, in the end, make these books "Victorian" after all. And fourth, it will attempt to elaborate these arguments by way of a preliminary consideration of the characteristics that themselves become conventions or are responses to earlier conventions, the accumulation of which gives that sense of "family resemblance" that allows us to identify the distinctively Victorian character of these novels. In a final chapter, the book will examine with some care a single Victorian novel, *Middlemarch*, perhaps the greatest of them all, as it manifests in its encyclopedic range and its aesthetic richness the kinds of preoccupations, social, philosophical, ethical, and aesthetic, with which the book as a whole has been concerned.

IV

Victorian novels, however diverse, tend to share unevenly certain pre-occupations, certain methods of representation and of structuring narrative, certain ideological predispositions, certain notions of gender role and of class and of the nature of work and money and of the relation of all this to religion. Recognizing the characteristics that eventually lead readers to the intuition of family resemblances is one of the fundamental requirements for learning to reread Victorian fiction, learning to read it.

There is no possibility of providing a complete and foolproof list of these characteristics, but I want here to discuss some of the most important of them. In an ironic way that I have already suggested, these characteristics, appearing most often in novels that insist on their work of registering as precisely as possible the way things are out there in the real, not the literary, world, begin to feel like new literary conventions, the conventions of Victorian realism.

Michael McKeon has argued that "questions of truth," epistemological ones, and "questions of virtue," social ones, had everything to do with the generic instability that helped produce and sustain the novel as a form, and that, I would also argue, informed the qualities of the Victorian novel that I have been discussing thus far. McKeon claims convincingly that "the instability of generic categories registers an epistemological crisis, a major cultural transition in attitudes toward how to tell the truth in narrative" and that "The instability of social categories registers a cultural crisis in attitudes toward how the external social order is related to the internal, moral state of its members."[12]

There are few moments in the history of the West when both these categories, the epistemological and the social, were more pervasively chang-ing, and the Victorian novel is one of the most obvious symptoms of these transformations. Although it is always important to attend to the individual differences among novelists and novels, it is impossible not to notice across the vast range of Victorian fiction some widely shared assumptions, and some widely exploited devices, with which the novelists engaged the crises.

The enormous social, economic, intellectual, and political changes that reshaped the structures of power throughout Europe had become in the nineteenth century absolutely fundamental to the way most people lived and thought: technology and science were increasing mechanical power, diminishing distances, shifting populations and power from the country to the new cities, facilitating communication and, of course, transferring political authority. There is no need to dwell here on the usual facts about demographic and industrial changes in the course of the nineteenth century, or to reflect on the difference made by the railways or advances in printing or the development of hard industry in the North. It is clear that changes in material culture simply transformed life in Victorian England and in so doing transformed the way people could think about themselves and their relations to others. The transformation was destabilizing even on questions about how one gets to the truth and where one should look for ethical and spiritual authority. On the one hand, science was claiming absolute authority in the area of natural knowledge, but on the other, in displacing the authority of religion it also made truth a much more elusive quality. The peculiar qualities of the Victorian novel are certainly reflections of these transformations and instabilities, symptoms and agents of the culture's reimagination of itself. I will, in what follows, attempt to lay out some of the central characteristics of Victorian fiction as they relate to these social and epistemological crises.

Time, change, transition

One of the first things that is likely to strike a reader of Victorian novels is how self-consciously they register a sense of transition and change, following the growth of children to adulthood, noting the difference between North and South, between urban and pastoral, and indicating rapid movements among classes still sharply defined and distinguished. They persistently dramatize the instability of the relations among classes, and that instability is obviously a key to their class sensitivity. However cozy the worlds of Victorian fiction can seem (and they are often not cozy at all), they reflect a deep sense of instability everywhere, not only in class relations. They register the instability of a wide range of cultural norms, even the very conception of time. The rapidity of economic and intellectual change made it difficult not to think of one's moment as a moment in transit, moving from a stage-coach-slow-moving past to a railroad-fast present. Self-consciousness about time and history, reflected for example in Thomas Carlyle's influential book, *Past and Present* (1843), indicated how intensely different past and present seemed, but more important, how self-conscious about its own modernity Victorian writing tended to be.

The Victorian novel (often full of railroad travel) helped both register and create a new sense of time: on the one hand, the presentness of the present, with its economic and class fluctuations and the new urbanization and industrialization of the country, and on the other, the pastness of the past, which seemed slower, quieter, more picturesque, and much less busy. This has a quality of the self-evident about it, but the Victorians, it seems, really did create the past in a new way, as a dying time, as a time to be regarded with nostalgia, but also as a time that had to be transcended. And yet, the nostalgia for the past and the concern with continuity between past and present also provoked among the Victorians much concern about the loss of stability and certainty and about the pace of the transformation. George Eliot's novels are particularly concerned to resist the idea of radical and abrupt change because, she believed, while the past may well have been wrong about most things, to cut off the roots of oneself in that past would be to leave one aimless and destructive. Her "conservative-reforming" politics were built on the idea that change must come slowly and organically, not on the basis of merely intellectual pursuits, rapidly and mechanically.

Her organicism, her sense of the vitally connected nature of all things, has roots among the romantics and the Wordsworth and Scott whom she loved. Organicism tended to create a tension between knowledge and feeling, for she recognized that while the past might indeed have been mistaken, while Christianity was built on an erroneous belief in the divinity of Christ and the literal truth of the biblical text, the right move was not simply rejection. She insisted on what she called "truth of feeling," a truth that told her that a violent, revolutionary breaking away from old traditions and the people who believed in them would be simply destructive even if rationally justified. Change had to come through history, slowly, organically. And while George Eliot was, of course, exceptional among novelists in her philosophical sophistication, her basic sense of things is paralleled in the work of most of the major Victorian novelists.

Scott's *Waverley* (1814), the first of his novels, is subtitled *'Tis Sixty Years Since*, and a remarkable number of Victorian novels are set self-consciously a generation or two in the past, and in effect create the past as they imply that all characters are "historical," and that what is depends on what was. One of the reasons Scott's novels were so immensely popular is that they recreated – or created – an exotic but dangerous past, the primitive culture of the Scots Highlands, and a past that was at the same time wonderfully attractive. Yet they recorded, with something of relief and regret at the same time, the defeat of that past. As in *Waverley*, Scott leads his protagonist out of the dangers and beauties of the past into a much more recognizable and apparently normal bourgeois present and the domesticity of the modern world. That world, marked historically by the unification of England and Scotland, is distinctly unromantic, distinctly bourgeois, and able to look romantically and nostalgically back on the defeated Highlanders and the past just because they are no longer threatening. Much of the power of Scott's *Redgauntlet* (1824) – which, it must be admitted, was not very popular in Scott's time – derives from the ultimate ineffectualness of a last frail effort of the Jacobite rebellion, and from the disparity between Redgauntlet's potentially heroic demeanor and aspirations and the bathetic collapse of his efforts. The past becomes beautiful and fascinating, an occasion for nostalgia, at the same time as the utter inappropriateness and inefficacy of its heroic codes are made manifest. If, on the one hand, Scott's novels can be understood as an attempt to "save" a dying past, on the other they in effect create that past, and in narrating the conflict of cultures, of past and present, they become the instrument by which the transition to a more livable if less beautiful present is made to seem inevitable. Understanding Victorian novels depends in part on understanding the complicated historical work that Scott's novels did during the years just preceding the coronation of Queen Victoria.

History

Scott's novels might be taken as a symptom of the ambivalent response to the "questions of virtue" with which the Victorian novel was to be so intensely engaged. *Waverley* appeared in 1814; Waterloo happened in 1815. Napoleon (of whom Scott in fact wrote a biography) became a focal figure in the historical narrative that, for the nineteenth century, marked Europe's movement into the modern, and Waterloo marks yet another moment when "questions of virtue" destabilized tradition. Europe and England had changed radically in the course of the French Revolution, and Europe's obsession with Napoleon lasted through the century, perhaps climaxing in the twentieth century with Hardy's epic poem, *The Dynasts* (1904–8). England's triumph might be read (with several grains of salt, as any such allegorizing of history should be taken) as the critical moment that affirmed England's special power in Europe and the validity of its burgeoning bourgeois culture.

It is striking that Thackeray's *Vanity Fair* (1848), for the most part concerned with the fates of two girls seeking mates, for love or money, has as its precise center the Battle of Waterloo. Napoleon and Waterloo largely determine the fate of the main characters in the banality of their profoundly unhistorical lives, although Thackeray announces that "We do not claim to rank among the military novelists. Our place is with the non-combatants. When the decks are cleared for action we go below and wait meekly."[13] The position is perfectly anticipatory of the Victorian realist novel's relation to world-historical events. The present is recreated in Victorian fiction as the time of ordinariness, juxtaposed with the almost mythic stories of heroism and romance that fade like Redgauntlet's revolutionary ambitions. And it is just this insistence on ordinariness, against a more heroic and world-historical past, that gives a distinctive quality to Victorian realist novels. Although the focus of all Victorian realist novels tends to be on the Amelia Sedleys, the Maggie Tullivers, the Esther Summersons, world history almost always lurks around the corners from where these "slender vessels" live out their lives, although it is intimated rather than directly represented.

This "background" history is not merely an add-on in the expansive world of Victorian fiction, but rather a symptom of a widespread understanding that even personal identity is shaped by large social and historical forces, and it is difficult to disentangle the lives of characters from the conditions these produce, but of which they are, at best, only partially aware. While there are Victorian novels, like *Oliver Twist* (1837–8), that allow their protagonists to move through experience untouched and uncontaminated by the social or historical context with which they are much concerned, the full blown realist novel, like George Eliot's *Middlemarch* (1872), insists that "character is not cut in marble."[14] To understand character one needs also to understand the community in which it lives, the past that partly shaped it, the cultural values it has absorbed, or not; social conditions and the past have a great deal to do with who one is, how one acts, what one desires.

Class

One of the first things that strikes new readers of Victorian fiction is how almost preternaturally sensitive to class distinctions it is. Nowhere is the evidence of instability more clear than in the way Victorian fiction, though in a great variety of forms, treats the possibilities of movement between classes and the nuances of class distinction. The very understanding of character, the possibilities of plot, seem often to depend upon the questions of class hierarchy, the place each character occupies in the complicated social organisms in which they are shown to live. The shaping of the modern novel, from *Pamela* (1740) on, was certainly involved with the new porousness in class hierarchy that modernity brought with it. A book like *Vanity Fair* makes almost no sense without a firm grasp of the subtle distinctions of class on which much of the plot depends, but it is not only *Vanity Fair*. Narrators and characters within novels have an almost neurasthenic sensitivity to markers of class and to what sort of behavior is appropriate to each class. As James Eli Adams puts it, "The language and experience of social class become especially insistent themes in the novel in conjunction with new forms of social mobility in nineteenth-century Britain."[15] There are virtually no Victorian novels that do not imply the fundamental importance of class and do not make class a personal matter, something of which the characters are aware, something they have to fight or sustain. As class barriers become permeable and money becomes the most powerful instrument by which class distinctions were both broken down and erected, "romance" in the Victorian novel seems almost always entangled with class and money (as, we shall see, it is also often entangled with questions of vocation). It was true of *Pamela* in 1740 as it was of *Jane Eyre* in 1847. Even so remarkable an aberration from the Victorian norm as *Wuthering Heights* (1847) is structured around questions of class, Heathcliff's and Edgar's in critical contrast.

Vocation

The crisis of class permeability often worked itself out in yet another characteristic concern of Victorian fiction, its interest in the question of work – what work would the protagonist do? What sort of work is compatible with the dignity that class might have previously bestowed? How can one work in a competitive society without being corrupted in the struggle? Work comes to be the primary factor in establishing a character's very identity. While forms of comedy and romance are still evident enough in Victorian novels, the relation between hero and heroine was often defined by questions of work – without success in work it would be impossible to achieve the desired comic ending. Free floating orphan-protagonists must define themselves by finding a vocation. Alan Mintz has pointed out that for the Victorians

> A life begins when the passion for a certain calling is first discovered, and it ends when that passion is consummated or spent, and between there are the moments of apprenticeship, trial, and production. How the story ends may be different in each case, but the shape of a life as a coming-into-vocation remains clear.[16]

The pattern operates in novels as well as non-fictional biographies, and "vocation" – which carries over into capitalist modernity the echoes of earlier spiritual and ethical traditions – is a critical element in the defining of character and the unfolding of plot, so that in many Victorian novels, the romance, which is ostensibly the shaping force of the narrative, is in effect displaced by the quest for vocation. Or rather, romance and vocation become indistinguishable, as, for example, in Charlotte Brontë's *Villette*.

The term "vocation" is important also because it separates, or can separate, the question of work from the question of money. Work, or vocation, is no mere practical activity: it is a decisive ethical move, a move of self-definition. The literal secular problem for young Victorian protagonists is how they will be able to earn enough money to survive in a society in which all the traditions of trades and crafts and class have been disrupted. A question that echoes from novel to novel, from character to character, in book after book is, "What can I do?" "What can I do?" in the sense both of immediate response to dramatic situations, and of longer term meanings of making a living. The question almost always carries moral overtones. When Rosamond in *Middlemarch* asks Lydgate, "What can I do?" she is exculpating herself. Her point is that there's nothing she could have done and therefore she has not been morally culpable. When Dorothea asks, "What can I do?" it is a genuine plea for the opportunity to do something, an inquiry about what might be done to help. The novels themselves, asking "What can I do" about the protagonists, hover between these two ethically antithetical possibilities, but include a further ethical caveat. That is, whatever vocation the protagonist chooses it must be chosen for the sake of the work or for the sake of others, and absolutely *not* in order to make money – although, of course, the money is indispensable (and hence causes certain kinds of ambiguities with which the novelists must struggle).

Money

It is not a stretch to suggest that the implication of Victorian novels is that success and virtue go together only when money is *not* at issue. Novelists would, on the whole, likely have agreed with John Ruskin, who insisted in *Unto this Last* (1862) that profit is never (or should never be) the end of work. For each of the professions there must be some end for the fulfillment of which the professional would be willing to die. Even the merchant, Ruskin claims, should not be in business for the money: "the merchant's function . . . is to provide for the nation. It is no more his function to get profit for himself out of that provision than it is a clergyman's function to get his stipend." All "have a work to be done irrespective of fee."[17] Victorian novels, embroiling their protagonists in the complexities of society, may not always sustain so high a standard, and given their un-ideal representation of the difficulties of economic and social life, must somehow attend to the importance of money. But it is almost a diagnostic mark of Victorian fiction that its protagonists resist money, refuse it as a motive, turn it away. Very often, the novels get themselves out of difficulties – since there seems no way for the protagonists to get money without being compromised – by way of inheritance. Margaret Hale, in Elizabeth Gaskell's *North and South* (1855), inherits money from a friend of her father and rejoices that she can give all that money (officially "lend" it, since the hero could not accept a gift of money either) to the man she loves, who then can get his factory working again, though it had failed just because he was so honorable.

It is in the pursuit of worldly success that the protagonist is most vulnerable to moral failure. And it thus becomes critical – one of the most distinctive characteristics of Victorian fiction – that protagonists achieve worldly success without pursuing money directly. The social crises that the *Bildungsroman* tends to emblematize are crises both because the social order threatens to destabilize and because traditional moral values become in this context particularly fragile. In novel after novel there are tensions between the novelists' effort to keep the protagonists honest, and the other narrative impulse, to make sure that a comic ending, with worldly success bestowed, is possible. But the novel's tendency to depict life inside an expanding capitalist system often runs up against the traditional notion, built into conceptions of class hierarchy, that "money is the root of all evil." The very stability and structure of the novels are threatened by tensions of this kind, as in *North and South*, and, most obviously, in Dickens' *Little Dorrit* (1857). Can these novels convincingly, plausibly suggest that in the world, so minutely described, of modern social and economic intercourse there is a strong relation between merit and success? The comic form of early realist novels depends on a positive answer to this question.

It is taken for granted and rarely addressed directly that money is essential to successful life in the new society. It is also essential that the protagonist not be compromised in the pursuit. What matters – and here Ruskin's way of thinking is particularly relevant – should be the work itself, since focus on money for any but the very poor who need it simply to survive is corrupting and corrupt. For middle-class figures, like Amy Dorrit and Arthur Clennam in *Little Dorrit*, money is something of a curse. The happy comic ending is made possible by the fact that Amy ends up as impoverished as Arthur, a fact she gleefully announces to him while he sits forlorn in the debtors' prison, the Marshalsea, assuming that she is still rich. Honor would prohibit him from marrying her if she brought money along with herself to the wedding.

The *Bildungsroman* and the weak hero

A major Victorian subgenre with which stories concerned with vocation, work, and money are concerned is the *Bildungsroman*, which Franco Moretti calls "the 'symbolic form' of modernity."[18] Moretti argues that novelists concentrate on youth "because of its ability to *accentuate* modernity's dynamism and instability." It is in the Victorian novel that literature turns first and most intensely to the experience of childhood, and this turn is bound up with virtually all of the characteristics I have been discussing thus far. But the ideal emblematic figure is not only a child, but an orphan. Orphans are unconstrained by the conditions of their parents. They have to define themselves in the world as they grow, to choose which way to go, and their identities are not bound up with their traditional inheritances, of trade, or of social status. Orphanhood is the perfect condition for dramatizing the transition from the past to the present and of making inescapable the fact that in the new world, one has to define one's own direction, one's own selfhood, one's own place in society.

And one of the by-products of the Victorian novel's problematic relation to work and money is the notoriously weak male protagonist. This is a surprisingly widespread characteristic, beginning in Scott's *Waverley* again, a novel in which the titular hero, Waverley, while described as a dashing young man and a forceful, brave soldier, is in fact manipulated in the struggle between the Highlanders and the English and is almost always knocked out or imprisoned while the real battles are being waged. It is amazing, retrospectively, to consider how little Waverley does in the course of his many adventures. Ironically, the world is so powerful in its movements, and he so weak, that any action would compromise him absolutely. Absence of action ultimately allows him to get off the hook of guilt for participating in an insurrection, and Waverley's condition can be taken as a kind of emblem of the condition of the male *Bildung* protagonist, who may have Great Expectations, but who needs to renounce them in order to achieve moral success. Again, there is no weaker hero than Clennam in *Little Dorrit*, for he fails at everything important he tries to do, is persuaded into ruinous speculation, and ends in the debtors' prison, saved only by the poverty of Little Dorrit herself. And although on the margins of *Bleak House*, for example, there is an efficacious Alan Woodcourt who will eventually marry our heroine, in the midst of the novel the good men are peculiarly incompetent. Mr. Jarndyce, when confronted with trouble or with too much praise, simply withdraws. "The wind is in the East," he protests. Energy emerges only from the bad guys, like Krook and Smallweed. Even the remarkably efficient Inspector Bucket fails in his quest for Lady Dedlock – herself a "fallen" woman.

The female protagonist

Things are in fact quite different for female protagonists in Victorian novels. One of the characteristic marks of Victorian fiction is the very sharp awareness of gender difference. Crudely, one might say that male writers tend to depict women as "angels in the house" or "fallen." This cliché about the Victorian novel is certainly at least partly correct, but the novels themselves, sometimes constrained by dominant notions about women's irrationality, emotional sensitivity, maternal natures, capacity for quiet endurance, physical weakness, and so on, complicate the formula significantly. It is certainly true that the protagonists of the female *Bildungsroman* tend to be stronger, more in control of their destinies than heroes like Waverley or Clennam. In fact, the female *Bildungsroman*, just because it too is concerned with the question of "What can I do?" tends to work very differently from male versions. Jane Eyre must seek a vocation, a fact that for women has particularly strong class implications, and although she is threatened with a life of tedious secondariness, she resists the conventions of female behavior, resists oppression, and ends (some narrative trick, some god out of the machine is important here) entirely in control, even of the man whom she loves. Interestingly, David Copperfield is also threatened by oppression and degradation, but the novel deviates from his story for more than half its length and his own role in his fate seems remarkably passive – although of course his narrative insists that he works very hard as a writer and does achieve commercial success.

Nevertheless, the gender boundaries in Victorian novels are almost always sharply drawn. The limits on the possibilities of female behavior are deeply constricting. Charlotte Brontë's Lucy Snowe, in *Villette* (1853), develops a cold and austere language and way of being to protect herself from the constraints under which she must live, and from what she assumes will be deep disappointments. In order to understand adequately the ways in which Victorian novels work, it is crucial to understand the gender boundaries within which the characters can act (and which, for the most part, they officially accept). When Lucy Snowe dares to go out alone to cross over to Belgium to find work as a teacher she violates expectations about women's behavior. Recognizing the extremity of the action helps make sense of why M. Paul keeps talking about the repressed Lucy as though she were wild and daring. Similarly, in Anne Brontë's *The Tenant of Wildfell Hall* (1848), the reception of Helen Huntingdon, under the pseudonym of Mrs. Graham, when she moves to Wildfell Hall with nobody but her little boy and a maid, becomes immediately a focus for natives' curiosity and slander.

The women, however, particularly when written about by women, tend to be stronger, more active, more determining of their own fate than the male protagonists. That is partly because the women are usually *not* finding their vocation out in the thoroughly compromising world of business, where, despite Ruskin, the reigning objective was money. Their moral crises tend to have more to do with the possibility (or the perception) that they are breaking the moral norms for their sex than with the possibility of their having transgressed some serious moral norm in order to gain a living. It is only when sexuality looms that this sort of compromise becomes narratively crucial for women protagonists. One thinks, obviously, of the virtual "sale" of Louisa Gradgrind to Bounderby, in *Hard Times*

(1854), or of Gwendolen's marriage to Grandcourt in *Daniel Deronda* (1876), or, in quite another register, Becky Sharp's marriage to Rawdon Crawley in *Vanity Fair*. These kinds of marriage stories always incorporate questions of class into questions of romance, and always suggest, depending on whether the woman is coerced or, like Becky, eager, the moral as well as the practical limits of women's power to maneuver through modern society on their own.

Many of the characteristic moments in Victorian fiction derive from this sense of moral limits on women. One of the most common spurs to (extending) the plot in Victorian novels is the fact that it is absolutely impossible for the woman to take the initiative in a love relationship. Long pages of misunderstanding and talking around the issue slow down the conclusions of Victorian novels. Much of the last volume of *The Tenant of Wildfell Hall* (1848), for example, is given to this sort of delay and misunderstanding despite the fact that the reader knows without doubt that Helen and Gilbert love each other passionately. And one of the most powerful moments in all of Victorian fiction comes in *Villette* when Lucy, knowing that she may well lose M. Paul forever as he is being pushed away from her just before he goes overseas, finally cries out, "My heart will break." The intensity and significance of that outcry are comprehensible only if one has absorbed the sense of moral restrictions within which the lives of women are led in Victorian novels.

Moreover, given that the conventional thought is that the Victorian novel was absurdly nervous about sex, it is surprising to notice just how many Victorian novels are concerned with "fallen" women. Amanda Anderson has argued that the language with which fallenness is discussed in the Victorian novel suggests that the concern with sexual transgression is closely allied to a more general concern with control over one's self.[19] That is, a "fallen" woman "falls" away from the kinds of norms I have been talking about, and in so doing loses control of her character. This loss of control is juxtaposed with the Victorian ideal of willed and disciplined control which, Anderson says, allows characters to be "free." That is, maintaining control allows one to choose and thus to be free and responsible for one's choices. Losing control means that one's identity, insofar as one can locate it in its fallen condition, is not one's own at all, but is determined by one's environment.

The fallen woman is a particularly convenient foil for the Victorian concern with the nature/nurture question. Against this figure novelists tend to juxtapose characters, men as well as women, who by determination and strong will keep their characters in control. At which point, "A man's character is his fate."[20] In women's novels, the great struggle is to make it possible to say that a woman's character is her fate, and the Victorian novel as a whole, on the one hand emphasizing social and historical context, on the other insisting on the virtues of self-control and self-will, becomes a kind of battle ground over the nature/nurture debate.

Connections

Another aspect of the Victorian novel's response to new social conditions, including of course the extension of the reading public into the new middle class, was its tendency to expand its subject across classes in an almost encyclopedic manner. I have already pointed out how a critical issue, either overt or implicit, in these large, multiplot novels, is the question of "connection." The problem of connections, connected, as we have already seen, to the rapid economic and social transformations of the time, had formal consequences for the Victorian novel, most particularly in the multiplot novel. As class barriers became more permeable and cities grew at an astonishing pace, great numbers of people were living in near proximity while not even recognizing each other's existence. Victorian fiction would indeed pursue, in many different ways, that question of "what connection can there be" between the rich and the poor, the upper classes and the underclasses. *Pickwick Papers* (1837), that odd, comic, rambling first novel of Dickens, carries the reader from the comforts of middle-class life down to the dregs of the debtors' prison, and makes its narrative out of those often painful connections. As I will try to demonstrate in a later chapter, the very beginning of the Victorian novel can be understood to emerge, at least symbolically, from a scene in *Pickwick Papers* in which the protagonist must come to terms with the reality of the underclass. The epistemological problem (coming to know this other, dark reality) is absolutely entwined with the ethical problem (what to do once one recognizes that reality). The novelists' work is in part to bring the other reality to the attention of their readers. The multiplot novel, which normally traces at least two, and often more characters through parallel and occasionally intercrossing courses, registers something of this social upheaval, with its psychological and moral implications explored. In the course of this book, it will be useful to attend carefully to some of the more famous of these,

Vanity Fair to begin with, and, in a kind of summary analysis of Victorian motifs, *Middlemarch*.

Moral anthropology

Thus, the Victorian novel – which has in recent years often been treated as an ideologically retrograde form – became part of what might be considered a great anthropological undertaking, one that Henry Mayhew, with his amazing and revelatory work, *London Labour and the London Poor*, beginning in 1849, made more or less official. John Rosenberg describes the world that Mayhew depicts in a way that throws much light on the enterprise of the Victorian novel:

> The image of London that emerges from Mayhew's pages is that of a vast, ingeniously balanced mechanism in which each class subsists on the drippings and droppings of the stratum above, all the way from the rich, whom we scarcely glimpse, down to the deformed and starving, whom we see groping for bits of salvageable bone or decaying vegetables in the markets.[21]

In novel after novel, before Mayhew's work, which began in 1849, Dickens was exploring this strange, connected underworld. In his Preface to *Oliver Twist* (1838), Dickens defends his representation of the underworld of London in terms that anticipate and provide a rationale for Mayhew's non-fictional undertaking:

> I had read of thieves by the scores . . . but I had never met (outside of Hogarth) with the miserable reality. It appeared to me that to draw a knot of such associates in crime as really did exist; to paint them in all their deformity, in all their wretchedness, in all the squalid misery of their lives; to show them as they really are, for ever skulking uneasily through the dirtiest parts of life . . . it appeared to me that to do this, would be to attempt a something which was needed, and which would be a service to society.[22]

Dickens' justification is inflected with just that moralizing of realistic representation that became the hallmark of Victorian realism. "A service to society." In other novels, Dickens represents other aspects of that underworld, the "poverty" side of Mayhew's world, rather than the criminal side. But that too has a moral function.

The enterprise of introducing the nether world to middle-class readers and, as it were, teaching them not only *that* this nether world was there, but *how* one might best respond to it, was one of the great efforts of Victorian fiction. "The Condition of England Question" ran well beyond the newspapers and famous social commentaries by writers like Carlyle. For Elizabeth Gaskell, the anthropological work of the novel was often critical, most particularly in *Mary Barton* and *North and South*. In the latter, we have the characteristic romance plot bound up with the "anthropology" I have been discussing, as the narrative unfolds for the most part from the perspective of a middle-class woman from a pre-industrial South who must move to the bleak and colorless world of Northern industry. Anthropology and romance mix here, as they do in novel after novel, and the ideal union between the North and South becomes both the romantic and the moral conclusion. But once again, the subject is social transformation and the problem the novel tries to solve is the epistemological one of how to know it best. Gaskell does not offer a panoramic vision like Thackeray's in *Vanity Fair*, but while using a third person narrator she focuses the entire narrative through the eyes of Margaret Hale. Margaret serves in part as a stand in for the reader as Gaskell imagines the reader – someone who is in effect *from* the South and who has no experience of the sort of world, the North, in which the novel's main story is played out. The "anthropology" is, of course, personalized: it is not merely that Gaskell tries to inform the reader about that alien world that has become so important to the life of England, but that she wants to register the personal response, what knowing about this world *feels* like. Margaret thus becomes a mediator and the narrative moves her through the experience in a way that suggests the possibility of conciliation between the cultures of North and South. Representing the culture of the North subjectively, although with the guiding hand of the narrator just visible, re-enforces the empiricist commitment of Victorian fiction, but also helps to dramatize the fact that there are no absolute facts, that what can be known depends in great measure on what is felt.

The enterprise is characteristically Victorian then because the epistemological is also the ethical. The question is not only how can I get to know, how is it possible to avoid misunderstanding and miscommunication and misperception, but also what does one *do* once one knows. The task of the Victorian novelist, no matter how central to most fictions was the romance, was also to find a way to represent the transformation of society in a narrative form that might both illuminate and domesticate it. What would come to seem strange to modernist eyes is just the Victorian novel's strong impulse to move beyond the limits of a single story, to give to their fictions a social function.

The craft of Victorian fiction

The multiplot and panoramic novels of Victorian writers, the blockbuster volumes that bound together 18 months of parts publications, Trollope's wide ranging novels that replicate plots in different registers – these are not inevitably loose and baggy. It is true that the very format means that they cannot have the kind of concentrated attention to a single line of narrative that the Jamesian ideal of fiction would prefer. Certainly, they move – again controlled by the demands of the format – from one plot to another in the course of a 32 page installment, or, as with Trollope and Hardy, they develop different lines within the same geographical context across many long novels. It is important to recognize this not as failed art, but as art with a different kind of purpose and a different imagination of formal organizations. The various strategies by which these multiple and wide ranging volumes represent their worlds often, on close inspection, show themselves to be finely crafted. The craft of "echoes" from one narrative line to another – most famously in the parallel and antithetical stories of Rosamond and Dorothea in *Middlemarch* – suggests very clearly the degree to which Victorian writers, engaged in large social and ethical enterprises, were keenly alert to the "craft of fiction," though it was another kind of craft from the ones that James and the modernists most admired.

As I have been suggesting, questions of "virtue" in Victorian fiction are central and overt, and in this respect Victorian fiction tends to distinguish itself from modernist fiction. The old cliché that Victorian novels are terribly prudish, particularly in relation to continental fiction, has some truth in it, but it can be put in another way: Victorian novelists, no matter how much driven by forces of the market, tended to think of themselves as practicing a vocation, of writing with a deep social (*as well as* aesthetic) responsibility.

The moral did tend to take priority, but in the best novelists it was rarely uneasy or prudish, always complicated and difficult. For the Victorians, the moral was rarely unmixed with questions of "truth," and that question is in some ways even more complicated, and takes the reader beyond the overt subjects of the novel – social class, work, anthropology, the romance plot, for example. Victorian novels are marked by a remarkable variety of strategies of narration, each designed to register reality in a richer way. There is a famous passage of George Eliot's – one that in effect defines the "moral realism" that became the dominant literary mode of the period – that is impossible to ignore when approaching this aspect of Victorian fiction. In *Adam Bede* (1859) the narrator "pauses a little" to explain and justify the un-ideal nature of the book's subject. The narrator (still a "he" in *Adam Bede*) insists on the importance of describing things as they are, of describing the unpleasant, the unattractive, the ordinary, and she does so on moral grounds – "things may be lovable that are not altogether handsome, I hope," he says. Readers need to cope with the vulgar if there are vulgar things out there. "But let us love that other beauty too, which lies in no secret of proportion, but in the secret of deep human sympathy."

> In this world there are so many of these common, coarse people, who have no picturesque sentimental wretchedness! It is so needful we should remember their existence, else we may happen to leave them quite out of our religion and philosophy. . . . Therefore let Art always remind us of them; therefore let us always have men ready to give the loving pains of a life to the faithful representing of commonplace things . . . I want a great deal of these feelings for my everyday fellow-men.[23]

This passage is a kind of credo, a statement of faith in the kinds of sympathetic anthropology that we can find in Gaskell's work and in George Eliot's.

But the passage not only insists on what the subjects of novels should be; it implies something about the nature of truth itself. At the start of the chapter, the narrator asserts what his project is:

> I aspire to give no more than a faithful account of men and things as they have mirrored themselves in my mind. The mirror is doubtless defective; the outlines will sometimes be disturbed; the reflection faint or confused; but I feel as much bound to tell you, as precisely as I can, what that reflection is, as if I were in the witness-box narrating my experience on oath.

George Eliot was by far the most sophisticated theorist of the Victorian realist enterprise, but for her too, the ethical and the epistemological are tightly bound, and this complex has a powerful effect on her craft. She faces the difficulties of accurate representation conscious that her narratives thus require particular attention to how they are told and how they are structured. She makes explicit what is often implicit in Victorian fiction, that "the mirror is doubtless defective," and consciousness of limitation often marks Victorian realism despite the fact that the traditional view has been that the Victorians wrote as if they had some unmediated connection with their subjects. But the sense of limits intensifies for George Eliot the responsibility to work as hard as possible to get it right, and increases the seriousness and responsibility of the enterprise of writing novels. The metaphor she uses here makes clear the solemnity of the responsibility – George Eliot writes as though under oath in court. Her commitment to accurate representation of what is mirrored in her mind (and of course, one must notice that she does *not* say she is describing the thing, but only how the thing impresses her) is a moral commitment to tell the truth. It implies a radically empiricist epistemology: one can only know what one experiences; truth telling is the act of describing one's experience as accurately as possible. But doing that requires attention to the way the mind perceives the "truth," and organizes it.

All of this implies an absolute commitment to the faithful recording of things as they can be perceived, to the realist enterprise (as Victorian writers were to understand it). It means, within the category of epistemology that McKeon invokes, that the writer is committed to finding ways to represent the world accurately; and that, it turns out, though more or less possible, is no easy enterprise. While Victorian fiction is usually thought of as dominated by omniscient narration, by the voice of an all knowing narrator, omniscience itself can be very various. There are many variations in the Victorian pursuit of the right sort of narrator, the right way to represent the experience to be narrated. Wilkie Collins famously played around with stories that are patched together with the personal narrations of many characters, while there is no voice of the author anywhere to be found. And it was during this period that free indirect discourse was most fully developed, obviously by Henry James, but before him in particular by George Eliot herself.

With all of this said, it is certain that this catalogue of characteristic elements of Victorian fiction is hardly complete. A thorough study of the Victorian novel would have to take into consideration, for example, the way in which empire occupies the margins of these narratives, ostensibly so provincially focused on the life of the British Isles, and so scrupulously minimizing both England's relation to Europe and other nations (and carefully avoiding overt connections with continental writing) and its relations with the empire, from which, for example, Bertha Mason comes, the moonstone is stolen, and Joss Sedley's wealth is gathered.

The Victorian novel has a complex and sometimes almost secretively disguised relation to the empire, and any reading of Victorian novels should finally come to terms with this complexity and recognize the way in which Empire – and continental culture, as well – work in the destabilizing of traditional culture that operates in so many significant ways in the novels. Empire manifests itself overtly and insistently only at the end of the Victorian period, although it hovered around the edges of a re-markable number of classic, and seemingly provincially English, novels. Given the scope of this book, unfortunately, the implied empire of so many Victorian novels will not be much discussed, but it is important to attend to Edward Said's argument that "stories are at the heart of what explorers and novelists say about strange regions of the world; they also become the method colonized people use to assert their own identity and the existence of their own history."[24] Said goes on to read books like *Great Expectations* into colonial history, and read back into European culture, the stories that colonized people have told about themselves.

The Victorian novel is, as I have suggested, too large to be contained by any formula of definition, by any calendar of characteristics, but recogniz-ing the kinds of issues that emerge out of the epistemological and ethical transformations that mark Victorian culture should help significantly both to complicate and to enrich our understanding of the remarkable novels that we will want to label, after all, Victorian.

Notes

1   See Robert Alter, *Partial Magic: The Novel as a Self-Conscious Genre* (Berkeley: University of California Press, 1975).

2   The most explicit and extensive version of this kind of argument comes in Robert Garis, *The Dickens Theater: A Reassessmment of the Novels* (Oxford: Clarendon Press, 1965). Garis argued that Dickens' great achievement was indeed to be theatrical, entertaining, and that his moral seriousness and formal powers were

largely irrelevant to his real achievement. Garis's arguments have in recent years largely been dismissed, but insofar as they emphasize how insistently entertaining Dickens tried to be, how engaging he tried to be to a wide audience, they have some salutary implications.

3   Virginia Woolf, "George Eliot," in *The Common Reader*, 1st series (New York: Harcourt, Brace and Janovich, 1953), p. 172.

4   Franco Moretti, *The Way of the World* (London: Verso, 1983), p. 214.

5   Jane Austen, *Northanger Abbey* (1818), ch. 5.

6   See George Eliot's essay, "Silly Novels by Lady Novelists," originally published in the *Westminster Review* (October, 1856), reprinted in *Essays of George Eliot*, ed. Thomas Pinney (New York: Columbia University Press, 1963), pp. 300–24.

7   For important discussions of the way forms of publication were related to the substance and form of the novels themselves, see Norman Feltes, *Literary Capital and the Late Victorian Novel* (Madison: University of Wisconsin Press, 1993), John Sutherland, *Victorian Novelists and Publishers* (London: Athlone Press, 1976), and Kathleen Tillotson and John Butt, *Dickens at Work* (London: Methuen, 1963).

8   John Henry Raleigh, "What Scott Meant to the Victorians," *Victorian Studies* 7 (1963), 7–34.

9   Alexander Welsh, *The Hero of the Waverley Novels* (Princeton: Princeton University Press 1992).

10 The most distinguished of these is D. A. Miller, *The Novel and the Police* (Berkeley: University of California Press, 1988). See also Lennard Davis, *Resisting Novels* (New York: Methuen, 1987).

11 Cervantes, *Don Quixote*, I (1605), ch. 6.

12 See Michael McKeon, *The Origins of the English Novel, 1600–1740* (Baltimore: Johns Hopkins University Press, 1987), in which this argument is most extensively developed. The quotation is taken from McKeon's important anthology, *Theory of the Novel: A Historical Approach* (Baltimore: Johns Hopkins University Press, 2000), p. 383.

13 Thackeray, *Vanity Fair* (1848), ch. 30.

14 George Eliot, *Middlemarch*, ch. 72.

15 James Eli Adams, "Class in the Victorian Novel." In Frances O'Gorman, *Companion to the Victorian Novel* (Oxford: Blackwell, 2004), p. 48.

16 Alan Mintz, *George Eliot and the Novel of Vocation* (Cambridge, MA: Harvard University Press, 1978), p. 21.

17 John Ruskin *Unto this Last: Four Essays on the First Principles of Political Economy* (Lincoln: University of Nebraska Press, 1967; 1862), p. 25.

18 Moretti, *The Way of the World*, p. 5.

19 Amanda Anderson, *Tainted Souls and Painted Faces: The Rhetoric of Fallenness in Victorian Culture* (Ithaca: Cornell University Press, 1993).

20 As we shall see in chapter 4, this dominant view was partly challenged by the sensation novel. Novalis's aphorism is repeated in many novels, most famously, George Eliot's *The Mill on the Floss* (1861).

21 John Rosenberg, introduction to Henry Mayhew, *London Labour and the London Poor* (New York: Dover Publications, 1968), p. v.
22 Charles Dickens, *Oliver Twist*, Preface.
23 *Adam Bede* (1859), ch. 17.
24 Edward Said, *Culture and Imperialism* (New York: Alfred A. Knopf, 1993), p. xii.

Chapter 2

The Beginnings and *Pickwick*

To get a good sense of what it is about Victorian fiction that distinguishes it and that gives it that odd quality of apparent accessibility and quiet difficulty, it will be useful to understand something of the historical conditions under which it was produced. A particularly convenient way to do that is by looking at the novel that made the reputation of the first great Victorian novelist, Charles Dickens. That novel, of course, is *The Pickwick Papers*, first published in 20 installments, from March 1836 to October 1837, and then in one volume, the parts bound, in November 1837. Conveniently, 1837 was also the year of Victoria's coronation, so that Dickens' novel has both a representative and literal significance. It does literally initiate the Victorian novel as we have come to know it, and it is strikingly representative of the kinds of preoccupations that mark the development of the novel through the nineteenth century, of the shape it took, of the subjects it engaged, and of its framing assumptions.

The point of this chapter is not to offer a "reading" of the book, but to introduce some of the fundamental aspects of Victorian novel publication and their relation to formal, artistic, and thematic emphases in the novels themselves. When, in his opening comment on *The Pickwick Papers*, John Sutherland boldly asserts that it is "The most important single novel of the Victorian Era,"[1] he is not eccentrically hyping a peculiar favorite of his. Nor, however, is he arguing that it is the "greatest," the most brilliantly constructed, or the most powerful of Victorian novels. But he is claiming that it was truly groundbreaking and enormously influential even though nobody was to succeed in writing another book just like it.

Of course, as the book that quite literally made Dickens an international success, it has its own special interest, in particular because in it we can watch the novel discovering itself as a novel, and in doing so, anticipate the whole genre, both structurally and thematically. It is particularly appropriate as an introduction to the Victorian novel in that it was so extraordinarily popular: it reminds us that the Victorian novel, whatever else it might have been, was almost universally conceived as a popular entertainment, designed to appeal directly to a broad (and expanding) middle-class audience, who might recognize in it their own world, learn better how to maneuver in that world, sympathize with its protagonists, and attempt to emulate its ideals.[2]

Pickwick, barely a novel at all, unfolds those attitudes, preoccupations, contexts, subjects, and themes that would become central, in various ways, to Victorian fiction. Up until *Pickwick*, Dickens had published only *Sketches by 'Boz'* (1835–6) which, as the name suggests, was a series of short "sketches" and stories. *Pickwick*, which itself began rather like a series of sketches, contractually required a very long story, one that would stretch over more than a year and a half of substantial monthly publication. In one sense, one might say that the business arrangements to which Dickens agreed when he undertook the book were the real engine for the development of the Victorian novel! Dickens' genius responded to the constraints.

He explains, in his Preface to the Cheap Edition of 1847, that he was offered the job of writing supporting text for monthly publication of a series of comic sporting illustrations by the well-known but then largely out of pocket artist, Robert Seymour, at £14 a month, 24 pages to go with 4 sketches. The tradition of "sporting sketches" was well established by that time, and Dickens was to be – on the basis of the success of his early "Sketches" – a hired hand in the production. But he insisted that if he were to do it, the priority would have to be reversed: the sketches would have to grow from the writing, rather than, as in the past, the writing from the pictures. His proposal was agreed upon, and, as Dickens was to put it, in what turns out to be a momentous sentence, "My views being deferred to, I thought of Pickwick."[3] Shortly thereafter, having finished most of the drawings for the first two of the twenty proposed monthly installments, Seymour – already a very anxious and unhappy man, but perhaps further harried by Dickens' demands and independence of creative energy – committed suicide. Dickens took virtually complete control of the publication from then on. Immediately the amount of writing for each number was increased and the number of illustrations cut in half.

Like Seymour, Dickens was interested in capturing a large audience while at the same time avoiding being branded as a mere popularizer – serial publication of this sort had been considered up to then a low and cheap form of publication. But however serious and "high" Dickens aspired to be, *Pickwick* was first of all an enormous popular success (though not until after a few installments). *Pickwick* gave evidence, moreover, that writing literature was – whatever else it might be or become – a job, a way of making a living, and signaled that the novel would be a form of literature that was open to writers outside the cultured male elite, middle-class or aristocratic, Oxbridge circle. Writing novels like *Pickwick* did not require a classical education, or training in rhetoric; it required only the power to make something interesting out of the recognizable conditions of contemporary middle-class life. Well, certainly, its enormous success depended on Dickens' extraordinary imagination and linguistic virtuosity, but these were not the product of formal education. The book was the creation of a particular moment under particular conditions, and the moment saturates the novel.

Considering the centrality of the contractual initiation of the novel and the importance to the young and aspiring Dickens of selling a lot of copies can only re-enforce the point that the Victorian novel, as a now recognizable form of art, grew out of a new economic and social order, primarily through writers who wrote "for money," as Samuel Johnson assumed all but fools did. Despite the history of eighteenth-century fiction, in which the young Dickens was steeped, and despite Henry Fielding's efforts to give to his novels that quality of education and artfulness that might mark them off from the merely popular and give the form a classic heritage, the early nineteenth-century novel made no pretensions to being great art. It did not invoke the muses as it plunged into its narratives about contemporary life, about people who lived in conditions immediately recognizable to readers, and who struggled against the very conditions that determined their lives.

Dickens was a member of an economically marginal middle-class family which, at one point, went bankrupt. The familiar story is that, facing poverty, his parents sent him to work in a blacking factory – something for which he never forgave them, as is testified by so many inadequate mothers and fathers in his novels. This apparently very personal experience tapped into a central concern of his nineteenth-century public, for the question of "class" was to dominate much, even most, Victorian fiction, and Dickens' real and imaginative energy was devoted to defending his class position, defining its qualities, and resenting those who threatened it. When the aristocracy emerges in most Dickens novels, particularly in the early ones, it is not a pretty picture. *Pickwick*, by and large, stays away from the aristocracy, but provides some of the most uproariously funny sequences in all of English literature in its depiction of social climbing, most particularly, the soiree of Mrs. Leo Hunter, who aspires to know only distinguished people and who writes very strange poetry indeed (ch. 15), or the soiree of "a select company of Bath footmen," mocked and exploited brilliantly by Sam Weller, whose virtue is, among other things, that he sees through all pretensions (ch. 36). But whether the aristocracy is present or not, Dickens' work is almost hypersensitive to questions of class, and his attitude toward social pretension and aristocracy is not far from Sam Weller's, after all.

The form of the novel that gave Dickens his position among Victorian novelists reflected just these kinds of issues. Monthly installments, priced at one shilling, allowed most middle-class readers access to books, whose price fully bound was often beyond their reach. While a shilling certainly was a lot more substantial than it sounds to modern ears, it was, once a month, at least manageable for most middle-class families; for those "below stairs," shared copies or readings aloud meant an even wider non-elite audience for Dickens than the sale of the monthly installments suggests. Although the 20 part novel was not the only form of Victorian novel publication, by any means, serial publication in one form or other was to become a staple, and while audiences varied depending on the venue (during the Victorian period new journals devoted largely to the serial publication of novels sprang up for differing audiences), the long narrative slowly played out across long periods of time was to become a distinctly Victorian phenomenon. Serial publication, moreover, precluded the kind of artistic control of the whole that novelists who write and rewrite their novels before publication possess. Dickens is notorious for having written down to the last moment, when the printer's boy would rush over to pick up copy for the next installments.

There was another form of novel publication that became very popular during the period, not quite serialization, but with as powerful an effect on the nature of the novel. From the 1840s onward, Victorian fiction publishing was significantly influenced by the lending library, the most powerful of which was Mudie's, which offered annual subscriptions and found that the most profitable kind of volume was the famous "three-decker." Three deckers were published in three volumes and were particularly profitable to the libraries because each volume could be rented out separately and thus any novel could service three different readers at the same time. The lending library's economic power was so great that it could virtually censor the content of the books it circulated and determine the size of novels that publishers would agree to publish. Serial publication and the pressure of the lending libraries guaranteed that a large number of Victorian novels would be very long and compendious. The marketplace is always a player in Victorian fiction.

There were variations played on these forms of publication. Dickens, for example, edited two journals over many years, *Household Words* and then *All the Year Round*. Those journals, but particularly the latter, published novels in short weekly installments, a method that intensified the way forms of publication affected the actual structures and even themes of novels.[4] George Eliot, at the point in her career at which she had achieved great popularity with the public and deep intellectual respect, decided to publish her greatest work, *Middlemarch*, in half-volume numbers. Because she was discovering that her treatment required a larger book than she had intended, she realized that she could not satisfactorily publish the book in the three-decker form, and was eager to escape the cheapening she thought parts publication produced, particularly weekly parts publication. George Lewes, her partner, made the arrangements with her publisher Blackwoods, and despite her aversion to the process began publishing some time before she had finished the whole thing. She began publishing the book in installments separated by two months, and remained at least one "book" ahead of the publication pace. Each installment was a substantial chunk of the book, and sold at five shillings (of which George Eliot received two).[5] Even George Eliot, then, who had so strong a sense of organic form and of the integrity of the work of art, was forced on occasion to manipulate her narrative to meet the commercial needs of publication. The Victorian novel, then, while it produced some of the greatest works in the canon of English literature, was very much also a product of commercial forces; its form, its subject, its very existence, tended to depend on the pressures for publication coming both from an expanding reading public, and from the publishers who serviced it.

How novelists imagined their narratives was virtually always deeply influenced by these publishing conditions and, through those conditions, by the popular preferences of the reading public. Money, one of the dominant elements of most Victorian novels, was almost always a significant theme of the novels and at the same time a significant part of the motive for writing. Certainly, Dickens used his "art" to work his way back substantially into the middle class, and however seriously he was to take his work, writing for him was first of all a means to a good living. Readers of Victorian fiction need to get comfortable with the economic emphases and energies that environ and give substance to the novels. The modern prejudice (which Trollope already derided) that assumes that writing for money is incompatible with serious writing does not operate forcefully inside the world of Victorian fiction-writing. Simply put, Dickens wrote to make a living. Despite objections, despite worries about writing that simply pandered to public taste, there was little in Victorian culture that allowed for the sharp division between "high" and "low" literature that was to intensify with the development of modernism and that remains in place even now, despite the messy emergence of a post-modernism that happily scrambles high and low, pop and traditional art.

The Victorian novel was, then, open to virtually anyone who could write, and many of its greatest works were produced by impecunious middle-class men and women. It is no accident that the Victorian novel is probably the first major literary enterprise in England in which a significant proportion of the most important work was done by women, in which the dominant proportion was written by people who had never attended the major, Oxbridge, universities. Anthony Trollope's insistence in his autobiography on the sheerly practical function of novel-writing and his famous analogy of the novelist to a shoemaker, though it was to disturb Henry James and to diminish Trollope's reputation among intellectuals at the end of the century, spoke a truth that helps at the same time explain the peculiar power of the Victorian novel to appeal to its new audiences.

But with class and economics and the material conditions of production so significant for the early Victorian novel, just what kind of book emerged out of these particular and peculiar historical circumstances? *Pickwick Papers* clearly began not knowing what it was to be. The invention of the Pickwick Club and the device of the quest for "scientific" knowledge provide the only plot, and the impetus to movements. The introduction of the startling and inventive Mr. Jingle in a very early chapter allows a somewhat richer variation of episodes, largely leaving behind the mock-science, but by and large, even with Mr. Jingle, the shape of the plot depends on the question, "Where should we go next?" It thus plugged into the tradition of episodic narrative that marks a wide variety of types – the medieval romance, the picaresque (rogue's story), the quixotic romance, and, of course, the sporting papers, which gave it its start, and, through them, to the episodic, picaresque romance tradition that traces the adventures of a traveling protagonist, with little attention to narrative development. The pleasure of such books tends to lie in the comedy, burlesque, excitement, and adventure of individual episodes, and not in the psychological or thematic development of character and plot. Dickens loved Tobias Smollett, who was both a translator of *Don Quixote* and the author of an amusing eighteenth-century variant on the picaresque, *Humphrey Clinker*, although Humphrey is no "picaro," but then, neither is Don Quixote, who aspires to the condition of the knight errant of medieval romance.

One immediate difference in *Pickwick* from its predecessors in any of the variations of this tradition is immediately noticeable. The rough edges are gone. The delight in scabrous misadventures or in excess violence, the sort of thing one might have got from the great predecessors like *Lazarillo de Tormes* or, more classically, *Don Quixote*, are toned down so that the worst of the violence and the villainy in the early chapters comes from Mr. Jingle, or the pugnacious cab driver who thinks Pickwick is spying on him, or the utterly innocent, apparently eighteenth-century style misadventures when Pickwick loses himself in the corridors of the inn and ends up in the wrong bed. These are funny enough, to be sure. But it is as if all the dirt had been swept away, and while these passages are descendants of far rougher and coarser episodes, there is nothing in them to offend a tidily conservative new middle-class family. As Dickens put it in the Preface to the 1838 edition: "throughout this book, no incident or expression occurs which could call a blush into the most delicate cheek or wound the feelings of the most sensitive person" (p. 7).

Posterity has often regarded this sentence with cynical superiority. Just this sort of absurd middle-class sensitivity to Mrs. Grundy is what kept the English Victorian novel from achieving the hard realist grit and then the artful glitter of continental, particularly French, fiction. But the attitude Dickens expresses in his Preface, whether accepted with total satisfaction or with a sense of the necessity of deferring to the crowd, hovers over the whole tradition of Victorian novel-writing, even where it is clear the novelist wants to burst free of the restraints. George Meredith's famous obscurity surely owes something to the implicit moral tightening that seems to restrain Victorian fiction; Thackeray's quiet cynicism and late aesthetic fatigue seem linked to his sense that while the world is as self-interested as Becky Sharp shows it to be, it is impossible to portray it without participating in it. It is not that there is no sexual hanky-panky, no seduction, no violence in Victorian fiction. Such things are almost always there, or at least just around the corner. The problem is that they are represented so cautiously, without making the innocent blush and without suggesting in any way resistance to the moral order. Famously, in the book he began writing and publishing in shorter parts even before *Pickwick* was completed, *Oliver Twist*, Dickens not only represents the brutal murder of Nancy by Sikes, but forces the reader, for however brief a moment, inside the criminal experience. *Oliver Twist* is less gentle spirited than *Pickwick*, and implies the possibility of a much darker view of the world, but the persistent innocence of its protagonist and the shape of the narrative itself fend off the dark shadows of illegitimacy, criminality, murder, and sexual domination.

Yet in the Victorian novel, the threat of just that sort of violence, or of the sexuality implicit in Arthur Donnithorne's behavior with Hetty Sorrel in *Adam Bede*, or the Princess Neroni's sexual play in Trollope's *Barchester Towers*, or Edith Dombey's flirtation with adultery, or even Richard Feverel's quasi-seduction, is contained and redeemed in various and complex ways. Years ago, Steven Marcus captured finely the special quality of Dickens' handling of blushworthy subjects, juxtaposing Dickens' art with the traditions of Regency England into which he was in fact born. Using virtually the same kinds of incidents that he found in Fielding and Smollet, Dickens, Marcus notes,

> has expunged every trace of the bawdy joke, has deleted the conventional observations of Smollet and Fielding about 'withered posteriors' and the like, and has substituted for the coarse directness of his predecessors a gentler kind of humor, emphasizing sentiments necessary to the comedy – the large generalized feelings of relaxation, fellowship and pride in individuality – as much as the comedy itself.[6]

Just such cleaning up is notoriously an aspect of virtually all Victorian literature, which is recognizably different from the "realism" that was growing up across the channel. The cleaning up of public discourse as it responded to the new moral order of the new bourgeoisie is a mark of the Victorian novel. In *Pickwick* it is done brilliantly, not only in separate incidents of the kind I've point to already, but in the whole conception of the central character and of the way he achieves his peculiar Dickensian happy moral heroism. After all, the raw outlines of Pickwick's story might justify the idea that he is only a dirty old man. Not only is he caught in the wrong bed, but he is caught too in the convent garden, and the entire novel spins around his being caught with Mrs. Bardell, fainted, in his arms: even his good friends suspect that something sexual must have been going on. Yet the conventions of sexual horse play common to the eighteenth-century novel are exploited here to emphasize Pickwick's absolute innocence. The threat of sexuality or deadly violence is moved way off center stage, as it is in most Victorian fiction, or it is treated with a delicacy that raw realism would not indulge. (The development, somewhat later, of "sensation fiction" requires particular and separate attention.)

Dickens was not only satisfying the demands of a new expanded reading public willing to shell out a shilling a month for amusement, he was – as many recent commentators have insisted – creating the taste for a new kind of bourgeois amusement and, as it were, teaching the bourgeoisie how to be, and how to behave. D. A. Miller argues that *"Oliver Twist* suggests that the story of the Novel is essentially the story of an active regulation."[7]

Pickwick Papers is not self-evidently at work regulating. But it is probably unique in Dickens' work and in the roll call of Victorian fiction in the degree to which the qualities of innocence and the refusal of worldly cynicism are not only represented but also thematized as an ideal to which we should all aspire. At the end of his Preface to the first bound edition of the novel, Dickens claims that he would be satisfied if it "should induce only one reader to think better of his fellow men, and to look upon the brighter and more kindly side of human nature" (p. 7). If there is "regulation" here, it is the regulation that comes with the willed choice to achieve Pickwickian ideals of generosity and self-sacrifice. The Victorian novel – and Dickens not least among its practitioners – would have to struggle with increasing difficulty to sustain such an objective. But however "dark" his novels became, and however threatened by cynicism and corruption, they aspire to a comic form, a form in which community and harmonious resolution of great difficulties are achieved. The Victorian novel usually attempts to represent a world in which the forces of self-interest, cynical struggle, and mere sensuality are not dominant, in which in fact they are "disciplined and punished." In the place of such self-interest, the novels imply (or optimistically incline toward) the possibility of real community – the ultimate aim of all romance – and loving resolution. Comedy was the form to which Victorian realism aspired (often, that is, just the reverse of the directions of continental realism), although it is achieved with increasing difficulty through the period, and in Dickens largely by force of ideal example. Marcus puts it well: "Without the gentling to which

45

Dickens submitted the conception of masculinity that he had received from Fielding and Smollet, the vision of innocence and benignity in *Pickwick Papers* could not have been realized. It was an achievement which had the immediate effect of adding to the novel what amounts to a new dimension of life." But he points out that "Seventy-five years later . . . a release of the material which Victorianism had suppressed was to have a revitalizing effect on the English novel."[8]

So what kind of book is *The Posthumous Papers of the Pickwick Club*? Since the book changes radically from start to finish, the question is a difficult one to answer simply. At the start it is a narrative that mixes interpolated, usually gothic tales, with light-hearted buffoonery and wit, as it moves from place to place and mock adventure to mock adventure. The premise, the inauguration of "The Corresponding Society of the Pickwick Club," to be composed of Pickwick, the "scientific" gentleman and author of a theory of "tittlebats," and three others more or less caricatured figures, whose conventional differences were to provide the greatest possibility, over the long haul of 20 months, for variations on diversions. Except for the remarkable invention of the comic villain Jingle, there seems no direction in the narrative but the desire to move about the English landscape searching for the funniest possibilities. Satirical, parodic, and deliberately without depth, the narrative would obviously have been difficult to sustain after a few installments.

Yet even these unpromising premises anticipate much that is central to later Victorian fiction. We might note, first of all, the determination to build the story around quite ordinary, if rather self-inflated characters, who, when treated with the high flown rhetoric of political journalism quickly become victims of satire and irony (and parody), qualities that have always been essential to realism. Whatever he will become in the course of the narrative, Mr. Pickwick is imagined at first primarily as a butt of jokes, a butt just because he is innocent, though at the start not a little vain. Juxtaposition of the innocent against practical worldliness is almost the founding trope of the modern novel – certainly it is the motive of the most famous of predecessors, *Don Quixote*. The Victorian realist novel attempts to represent, even in its most comic and optimistic forms, what would be called later on in the century the "harsh, unaccommodating, actual" as against the false imaginations of romantic aspirants. Realism cuts its teeth on this sort of assertion of itself against the romance energies that have traditionally driven narrative and that tend to represent characters ideally. Satire under these conditions is virtually impossible to escape.

The English realist novel, like *Don Quixote* before it, like Fielding in the eighteenth century, is much invested in irony, parody, satire. The ideal is exposed or belittled in the face of a practical reality. So the "papers" of the "Pickwick Club," which open and in fact provide the official title of the book, are written in the high public rhetoric of parliamentary reporting, of the sort of which Dickens himself was a master by that time, and there is even a kind of sophomoric excess, naming Pickwick "immortal" in the first sentence, and alluding to his "gigantic brain" on the second page. The triviality of the practices and the group being gathered for quasi-scientific investigation in travels around the country is a large part of the joke of the first paragraph. It is not, in the first chapters, a very sophisticated comedy, but it depends upon inflation of self-evidently ordinary characters and actions. There is an allusion to Pickwick's "Tittlebattian Theory," a move that mocks both Pickwick and the science that was gaining so much attention in early nineteenth-century England.

In usually very funny and even sophisticated ways, the novel plays off ideal against real, ideal against practicality, innocence against shrewd understanding, and at the start indulges just a touch of cynicism about the nature of Pickwickian innocence, which often seems more like stupidity than moral generosity. Thus, while *Pickwick Papers* is not the most obviously realist text, it goes immediately for the realist modes and themes.

The first major incident in the novel comes in Pickwick's encounter with the cabman, who responds to inquiries into his work and the nature of his horse with the sort of street wisdom for which Pickwick is absolutely unprepared. It is a gentle nineteenth-century version of some of the episodes in which Don Quixote thrusts himself into situations that end with his having his head smashed and suffering other humiliations and causing havoc, even moral havoc, just because he insists on reading experience as equivalent to the adventures of romance.

Such encounters do not always, in the Victorian novel, take the shape of comedy, but there is a great deal of it, for instance, in *Vanity Fair*, Becky Sharp being a very clever satirical writer in her own right. In mainstream Victorian narratives, plots are over and over again built around the juxtaposition of innocence with the worldliness into which it is thrust. The *Bildungsroman*, to which chapter four of this book devoted, is built on a kind of Pickwickian narrative, but the traveler is a young, probably romantically inclined innocent growing into and suffering the limits of realist constraints on his or her way to maturity. Jane Eyre, Pip (of *Great Expectations*), Thackeray's Pendennis, Maggie Tulliver (of *The Mill on the*

Floss), or Phyllis, in the lovely short novel of Elizabeth Gaskell's *Cousin Phyllis* – all of these young people work through narratives that juxtapose their innocence and romantic ambition against the constraints of the practical world.

The form of this juxtaposition is not always comic, but in the Victorian novel the kind of realism that builds upon the juxtaposition, for the purposes of contrast and satire, of the real and ideal, the dream and reality, becomes thematically central. The element of parody and juxtaposition of real and ideal, which is at first a matter for laughter, becomes in *Pickwick Papers* something quite serious, too, and almost turns the book into something very different from the warm and embracing comic narrative for which it is normally and fairly taken. In fact, *Pickwick Papers*, while achieving comic form, dramatizes the kinds of moral and social tensions that become central to the most serious Victorian novels. *Pickwick* is thus representative not only of the implicitly satirical elements in Victorian realist fiction, but of the tension in so many of the novels between the fundamental drive towards a comic resolution of problems and the force of the materials turned up along the way that threaten to make the narrative tragic or, at least, unhappy. *Pickwick* begins to incorporate into its very texture many more elements that anticipate many of the concerns and strategies of later Victorian novels.

To make this point it should suffice to consider two critical elements in the narrative. The first, significantly, is the point in the story at which the book clearly becomes a "novel," clearly develops a narrative direction, and begins developing Pickwick in a new way, making him, certainly, something more than the butt of jokes, and even when such a butt, a genial figure. There is no question that the appearance of Sam Weller in the novel corresponds to the moment at which monthly sales boomed and moved toward the astonishing number of 40,000. Sam, who in his relation to Pickwick, is a shrewd, cleaned-up, picaro-like equivalent of Sancho Panza in relation to the Don, changes the reader's relation to Pickwick in part because he is both so shrewd and at the same time so admiring of Pickwick's benevolent innocence.

And yet his introduction to the novel triggers the key events of the *Pickwick* plot. It is something more than a coincidence that Mrs. Bardell understands Pickwick's proposal to hire Sam as a proposal of marriage. "Do you think it's a much greater expense to keep two people, than to keep one?" he asks his landlady. There are obviously implicit issues about gender here – women, particularly in *Pickwick Papers*, do not seem very smart or capable and the narrative depends upon what the boys decide to do in their mateless rambles through England – but for this argument it should suffice to point out that Pickwick finds himself in what looks like a sexually compromised position just because he wants a "man." The novel in fact begins in this confusion, and the man that Pickwick is to hire becomes the counter-parody. That is, Sam works to protect Pickwick from the real world that, in his innocence, he doesn't understand. He thus transforms Pickwick from a rather silly butt of mild but awkward jokes, to an almost heroic innocent, whose inability to believe the worst of people and whose sheer capacity for joy in life exposes him to all sorts of nastiness and corruption, with which he will make no compromise. Pickwick's innocence grows into something almost mythic in character – as G. K. Chesterton long ago argued[9] – and turns the irony and satire away from him and onto the worldly-wise figures who attempt to exploit innocence, figured most prominently in the lawyers, Dodson and Fogg. And yet he does this, unlike the conniving Mr. Jingle, the first of Dickens' con-men, with a heart of gold. He has the shrewdness and wit of the picaro, the generosity and warmth of the protagonists of domestic fiction.

From this point in the narrative forward the novel becomes more consecutive. Nevertheless, a good part of the book, until the actual trial of Pickwick for breach of promise (occurring only in the eleventh monthly installment, in chapter 30), continues the rambling episodic, where-shall-we-go-next structure. After that point, the number of interpolated tales sinks drastically. And the texture of the narrative changes as well. At first, the narrative is largely related as it is supposed to be described in the "papers" of the Pickwick Club. By the middle of the book, the fiction of those "papers" is quietly dropped, and *Pickwick Papers* begins to become a characteristic Victorian novel, narrated by an "omniscient author." Moreover, it should be added, the substance of the narrative gets weightier, less like sightseeing and picaresque adventure. And it is a direct confrontation with this new weightiness that marks the second critical element in the transformation of *Pickwick Papers* into a novel.

For the suddenly increasing audience, Sam Weller was certainly the key attraction. But by protecting Pickwick, and after a minor defeat, triumphing over the less innocent with shrewd and bold moves worthy of the wickedest of them, Sam gives Pickwick the space to transform from the caricature he was at the start of the novel. Surely, Dickens didn't have anything quite so solemn in mind, but the figure of Sam in effect deals with the difficulty that Victorian novelists were to have throughout the life of that form – the difficulty of imagining a protagonist who was both active and capable and morally generous and – simply – good. The corrupting forces of the new society in which the new bourgeoisie were learning how to be bourgeois tended, under the eyes of observant writers, to stain almost every life, and the ideal of Victorian innocence, with which all later audiences are familiar, usually works out in a young woman who can remain unstained just because she is a woman.

The peculiarly attractive thing about Sam is that he has street smarts, and knows the ways of the world, and yet remains internally whole and generous. But even the purest of male Victorian protagonists has to learn to survive in the world of business, and rarely escapes unscathed. A catalogue of Dickens' own books would provide strong confirmation – *David Copperfield* brings Steerforth into Little Emily's life, Pip is corrupted by Magwich's money, John Harmon has to "be dead" in order to escape the taint of money, young Carstone is corrupted by "Jarndyce v. Jarndyce," and even Clennam in *Little Dorrit* succumbs to the temptation of the stock market. But the narrative of *Pickwick Papers* increasingly drives toward a full confrontation with the corruption that threatens Pickwickian sunshine, and at the point at which Pickwick loses the court case against him for breach of promise, he takes on heroic stature. He refuses to cave in to the brilliantly corrupt and nasty exploiters of innocence, Dodson and Fogg, and as a consequence (though it seems he could easily have paid the fine) allows himself to be cast into debtors' prison for what seems a sentence without term. It is a matter of principle. "'I beg to announce to you, my unalterable determination to pay no damages whatever,' said Mr. Pickwick most emphatically" (p. 410). When the negative verdict is in, Pickwick affirms to his lawyer that he will pay "not one halfpenny" (p. 468).

At which Sam cries out, "hoorroar for the principle, as the money-lender said ven he vouldn't renew the bill." The Wellerism is worth pausing over because it contains so much of the ambivalence that lay behind Victorian writers' confrontation with the new economy. It is, on the one hand, a satiric thrust, seeming to mock the "principle" that gives so much dignity to the irredeemably innocent Mr. Pickwick. But of course, Sam is fully sympathetic with his master even though he feels that it is entirely impractical for him to stand out for a little "principal" in the way of asserting his claim that justice is more important than practical comfort. He really is shouting hurrah for the "principle," but the irony is aimed at the "principal," at the money that is finally determinant of how the law and society operate. Sam knows this; Pickwick refuses to allow it. One way to think about this novel and about many Victorian novels is that, like Sam, they both know it and refuse it. The novel dramatizes the price of the "principle," and at the same time transforms Pickwick into a kind of heroic innocent. "A most extraordinary man that," says Mr. Perker (p. 541). In the Victorian novel, however, the slippage between "principle" and "principal" occurs frequently, sometimes to be thematized, sometimes to be disguised. One of the things that *Pickwick Papers* never does is talk about where Pickwick's money comes from or, in fact, how much he has. He can ramble so generously through the English landscape just because money seems to be no object to him. And a great part of the significance of his determining to go to jail rather than pay comes from the obvious fact that he could pay if he chose to ignore the "principle."

Inside the prison Pickwick is cast among the losers of his society, amongst a group of pathetic and ignoble figures of whose existence he barely knew before being jailed. "You don't really mean to say that human beings live down in these wretched dungeons?" (p. 544) asks Mr. Pickwick as he enters the Fleet for the first time. Pickwick is the first of Dickens' characters to be imprisoned for debt (as Dickens' father was imprisoned), but it is a theme that haunts his imagination. The potential horrors and humiliations of a society in which money rules so absolutely become part of Dickens' imagination and serve as a kind of dark projection of the evils and dangers of the new capitalist society that an innocent like Pickwick must come to understand and learn to cope with (and that, through *Pickwick Papers*, was about to give Dickens riches and fame). And although debtors' prison is not a literal presence in a great many Victorian novels, the threat of bankruptcy and debt hovers over an extraordinarily large proportion of those narratives. For Dickens, the climax of his preoccupation with this fate comes in *Little Dorrit*, the novel whose heroine was born in the Marshalsea and whose life and character are marked by that fact. In her character, principle becomes the central feature – and is constantly contrasted with principal, which is seen as everywhere debasing, corrupting, and dangerous.

Pickwick Papers' moral center is in the Fleet, for it is there that Pickwick must confront the grim reality he has managed to smile past, up until that point. There, for the only time in the book, Dickens finds it difficult to sustain the comic mode, and difficult to be playful. In the pre-Dodson and Fogg chapters, the worst form "evil" took was the devious, clever, word-playing Jingle's merciless exploitation of Rachael Wardle and his

mocking treatment of Pickwick and Mr. Wardle. The farce is more prominent than the moral implications. But the narrative that follows from
Dodson and Fogg's cynical exploitation of the law and that moves Pickwick
inside the Marshalsea grows increasingly dark and threatening – threatening to Pickwick, of course, but threatening too to the very comic mode of
which this novel becomes so extraordinary an exemplar. It is important
to note that within the narrative Dodson and Fogg go unpunished, successful representatives of a society that builds into its very legal processes
the ruthless pursuit of principal. But the novel grows darker yet.

The sequence in the Fleet climaxes with a remarkable moment that, in
its miniature way, announces a crisis within this new realist genre. Throughout the time of his imprisonment, Pickwick has been the mythic and
benevolent spirit that Chesterton described and that Sam admires. In
the critical chapter, Sam gives us the mythic divinity that Pickwick has
become, in a language that appropriately stumbles through lower-class
accent and poor grammar, but that carries with it a sentimental force that
transmutes the ordinary and the worse than ordinary into something larger
and more important (the task of Victorian realism throughout). To Job
Trotter, Sam insists:

> 'No vun serves him but me. And now ve're upon it, I'll let you into another
> secret beside that,' said Sam, as he paid for the beer. 'I never heerd, mind
> you, nor read of in story-books, nor see in picters, and angel in tights and
> gaiters – not even in spectacles, as I remember, though that may ha' been
> done for anythin' I know to the contrairey. But mark my vords, Job
> Trotter, he's a reg'lar thorough-bred angel for all that; and let me see the
> man as wenturs to tell me he knows a better vun.' (p. 608)

But angel though he be, he is powerless to change the world he now sees
with full clarity and horror for the first time. It is a world of degradation,
humiliation, and unjust law. It dehumanizes. And Pickwick sees it:

> There was the same squalor, the same turmoil and noise, the same general
> characteristics in every corner; in the best and the worst alike. The whole
> place seemed restless and troubled; and the people were crowding and flitting
> back and fro, like the shadows in an uneasy dream.

It is a powerful and a surprising moment. Surprising not because the
horrors are unexpected, but because they are rendered so intensely. To all
of it Pickwick now responds: "I have seen enough" (p. 610).

The innocent angel turns away from the realities of this humiliating life. The realist novelist cannot fail to represent that life. It is narrative crisis, and interestingly, Pickwick, out of love, not out of concern for himself, shortly after concedes defeat and pays the debt and leaves the prison. It is the fundamental compromise to which Victorian realist fiction must submit. There is no closing the door for the Victorian novel, which must find other strategies to extricate its comic narratives from the corruptions and stains of capitalist enterprise. Pickwick remained shut up all day. Even Sam couldn't "induce him to alter one jot of his inflexible resolution" (p. 610).

Pickwick Papers, then, anticipates even in its central development much that is characteristic of Victorian fiction, and while it introduces both to the reading public and to his range of characters shabby genteel and marginal middle-class figures, Dickens turns their world into a kind of magical and meaningful place, sustained by his brilliant manipulations of language and his remarkably energetic and daring imagination. The middle class enters his novels with a bang and a laugh, but exhibits itself as extraordinarily vulnerable to the very economy that produced it, and threatened by the wide world out there ready to break its moral rules. But *Pickwick Papers* also makes clear how rich the possibilities are for a non-elite literature to narrate the experiences of the non-elite and to find this often physically grubby work wonderfully funny and beautiful – and profitable.

Notes

1   John Sutherland, *The Stanford Companion to Victorian Fiction* (Palo Alto: Stanford University Press, 1989), p. 506.
2   The question of the relation of the modes of production of Victorian fiction to the actual "content" of the novels is addressed from a Marxist perspective by N. N. Feltes, *Modes of Production of Victorian Novels* (Chicago: University of Chicago Press, 1986). Feltes shows in convincing fashion how the historical conditions, not only of the particular deal Dickens made with his publisher, but of printing and publication at that moment, deeply shaped the nature of the book and help us account for its explosion of popularity.
3   For ease of reference, I am using here the Penguin edition of *Pickwick Papers* (London: Penguin Classics, 2003), p. 761.
4   See Norman Feltes's strongly Marxist argument that the very subjects of Victorian novels were their modes of production.

5 For a detailed and excellent consideration of the conditions of publication of *Middlemarch* and the way George Eliot shaped it, see Jerome Beaty, *Middlemarch from Notebook to Novel* (Urbana: University of Illinois Press, 1960).

6 Steven Marcus, *Dickens: From "Pickwick" to "Dombey"* (New York: Basic Books, 1965), pp. 23–4.

7 D. A. Miller, *The Novel and the Police* (Berkeley: University of California Press, 1988) p. 10.

8 Marcus, *Dickens*, p. 29.

9 See G. K. Chesterton, *"The Pickwick Papers,"* reprinted in George H. Ford and Lauriat Lane, Jr., *The Dickens Critics* (Ithaca: Cornell University Press, 1961), pp. 109–21.

Chapter 3

Vanity Fair and Victorian Realism

The dominant mode of Victorian fiction is "realism," although as we look back at Victorian novels from this long distance what was thought of as "realistic" then may seem a little antiquated, quaint, even fantastic now. Everyone who has read Victorian fiction is struck by how shy it is of direct confrontation with sexuality, for example, and how mild is the violence that will sometimes erupt in its pages. Moreover, if we pay attention we note that the attitudes implicit in the writers' relation to matters that are now everyday reading on the front pages of newspapers, and rather like candy in our daily doses of television action, video games, and films, are strikingly different and probably far more intense than our own. Sikes's murder of Nancy in *Oliver Twist*, for example, evokes from Dickens the kind of horror that we barely feel at news of a devastating Tsunami or the deaths of dozens of Iraqis and soldiers every day. Arthur Donnithorne's seduction of Hetty Sorrel, which makes the crisis of *Adam Bede* and leads to Arthur's self-banishment and Hetty's ultimate exile, would seem hardly the stuff of high drama in a world where scandal of every sort is the nightly entertainment of millions.

All of which is simply to emphasize the enormous cultural difference that separates us from the Victorians. To engage with Victorian realism entails a sustained act of moral and literary imagination, and the remarkable thing is that the works of writers like Dickens and George Eliot and Anthony Trollope and W. M. Thackeray have had so long a shelf life and have remained so entertaining (and, one would hope, so interesting) even into this age of high technology in communications and in weaponry. It is necessary, before getting an adequate feel for all that is at stake in these novels, to understand something more about what realism means generally and what it might have meant in the nineteenth century, and to recognize that – putting it mildly – the word is not unproblematic. Let's say that it is a word that constantly changes its significance, and that much of its significance depends both on the temporal context in which it is used and the past to which it almost always, implicitly, alludes critically. Moreover, the word implies a kind of epistemology – that is, it implies that literature and language can somehow have access to things as they are, and even this apparently commonsensical view has been challenged throughout history.

For early modern writers, the "realism" that emerged from the tail end of Victoria's reign at the turn of the twentieth century was a largely dead and unimaginative "copyism." Sophisticated early modernists like Henry James, Virginia Woolf, and James Joyce turned the focus of their art inside, finding reality not in the prosaic registering of external fact, but in the complex working of their protagonists' minds. For the modernists, Virginia Woolf's marvelous and famous essay, "Mr. Bennett and Mrs. Brown" (1924), brilliantly dramatizes the aesthetic (and psychological and even moral) inadequacy of realist attempts to register in all their particularity things as they are as opposed to finding ways into interiority and the mysteries of the self. But early modernism's dismissal of Victorian realism is itself a historical phenomenon that, in the interests of developing a new kind of art, missed the imaginative power and the historical novelty of the Victorians.

In the meantime, realism has struggled back, though in a considerably weakened form, and under the scrutiny of very skeptical eyes, to some of the respectability that it lost early in the twentieth century. What credit it had by the mid-twentieth century seemed to have been exhausted entirely by the radically anti-realist arguments of modern literary theory after the 1960s, when the very notion of representing "reality" in any credible way was taken as reprehensible (perhaps ideologically dangerous) naïveté, or simple bad faith.

For the postmodernists, some of the animus against realism can be traced in J. Hillis Miller's two important essays on George Eliot's *Middlemarch* and one on Dickens' *Sketches by 'Boz'*,[1] each of which meticulously argues, though in different ways, that reading these texts literally as coherent representations of reality misses almost entirely the way the language of the books works and the ultimate impossibility of realistic representation. Neither of the famous insistently realist texts turns out on Miller's account to be really realistic. Nor can any literary text be. Beyond the epistemological problems, realism, it is also often suggested in recent discussions, at least in its manifestation in English, is always an act of "containment," an effort at "naturalizing," and thus no disinterested rendering of things as they are but imaginations of ways of keeping things under control, fashioning them so as to exclude their disruptive possibilities. The contradictions and impossibilities that epistemological questioning exposes turn out to have large social and ideological implications, and from the perspective of most recent theory, not good implications.

But while the unreal quality of antique charm that for modern readers so many Victorian novels now emanate (leading to so many film and television costume drama versions of the famous novels) might seem to provide a strong example to support this argument, the great Victorian novels are closer to the bone, more deeply intelligent, and more artfully crafted than either modernists or most modern viewers quite allow. If it be true that realism as a full representation of the real must fail in any absolute sense, given the nature of the medium itself and the inevitable limits of human knowing and perspective, there are ways in which the efforts of realism – so brilliantly analyzed by Erich Auerbach as a strong democratizing force with roots as deep as the Bible and Homer, and so strongly defended by Georg Lukács – continue to matter and require not passive recording but strenuous art. Once the necessary demystifying takes place; once the limits of the mode are laid bare; once the epistemological and ideological problems and disguises are recognized, realism – and the Victorian version of it – remains an important, even a necessary mode of literary art.

Given the vastness of the topic and its general significance for Victorian art, I will limit myself here to considering a few of its important, characteristically recurrent elements. My examples will come primarily from *Vanity Fair*, one of the great classics of Victorian fiction. The aim will be, by looking at some representative fragments, not only to point out some of Victorian realism's characteristic qualities, but also to suggest its limits, difficulties, and peculiar power.

I

I will begin with certain more general questions; first, the way in which the word "realism" begs so many questions and remains so difficult to define with precision. It is not simply that literary "realism" descends from a strange, even paradoxical history, moving from what might well be called an absolute idealism that posits the reality of universals (and the implicit unreality of the particulars that we would now identify as the real), to empiricism, which claims that the only knowable reality is what we can "experience," and finally to a positivist dismissal of Platonic universals as "nonsense." Realism is in its very nature a paradoxical form. The more strenuously empiricism pushes against an epistemology that makes ideas more real than matter, that insists on (divinely) inherited knowledge, that gives first place to intuition and imagination, the more clear it becomes that realism always, more or less surreptitiously, still depends on the mind as much as on "external nature." Perhaps ironically, therefore, realism has always tended to contain (in both senses of the word) idealism of some form or other, threatening to slide into what emerged in its late nineteenth-century manifestations as an almost absolute solipsism, what Walter Pater called the thick wall of personality through which no real voice ever pierces. "Experience," it turns out, is always of one's sensations, not of the things out there that supposedly trigger them. The external turns out to be internal, and realism's increasing turn to interiority, to throwing the drama inside, as Henry James put it, is in one sense an epistemological inevitability, although there are less philosophical and literary forces at work in the novel's turn to individual consciousness as primary subject. Victorian realism was not just a record of external things; it was always concerned with the complications of the inner life; and as George Henry Lewes, mate of George Eliot, said, the opposite of realism is not idealism, but "falsism." Victorian realism descends directly from the poetry of William Wordsworth, which made the "ordinary" into the romantic, and made the true epic not warriors' adventures around the world, but the growth of the mind.

The paradox of realism's implication in idealism is matched by another one: realism, rather than being, what it sometimes has given itself to be, an anti-literary mode, or at least a mode that depends not on literary tradition but on the way the world is, is of necessity a thoroughly literary mode. The urge to reality takes shape, consistently, in response to literary precedent, to the "cloud-borne angels, . . . prophets, sibyls, and . . . the heroic warriors" against which George Eliot sets "an old woman bending over her flower pot." The realist novel is similarly antagonistic to the romantic heroines whom Charlotte Brontë exposes as empty vessels, and to the romantic resolution in marriage that Thackeray deromanticizes in

Dobbin's marriage to Amelia. In every gesture toward the real, in every mock-heroic simile, from Fielding through Thackeray and Trollope, there is an echo of some literature that has imagined a very different reality. We have already seen how satire initiates so comic a book as *Pickwick Papers*, and that satire harks back, as I have suggested, at least to *Don Quixote*, and becomes a kind of signature of realism. The mockery invests the old literary forms with a new importance and marks its own anti-literary procedures as self-consciously literary. The literariness is a mark of realism's necessary self-consciousness, but among the Victorians in particular, it tends to be driven by a strong moral impulse (as well as an aesthetic one). For the realist, there is a lot at stake in getting it right, in telling the "truth," and it is no accident that realism tended to be the dominant narrative mode of a Victorian England in which perhaps the greatest of all virtues, greater than sexual propriety, was truth-telling. Observing things as they are, even with quasi-scientific detachment, displaces false representations with authentic ones, and forces us, as readers, out of the kinds of delusions that lead to moral disaster – Don Quixote's, or Emma Woodhouse's, or Emma Bovary's, or Pip's, or even Amelia Sedley's, for she, though innocent, makes a fantasy of her lover and then husband, and, were it not for good old Dobbin, would permanently have ruined her life and the lives of others around her.

While realism has a general reputation for being daring, even excessive, in its exposure of the terrible things going on just around the corner, it has – and again, this is particularly intense among the Victorians – an element of earlier kinds of narratives, exemplary tales, for example, or allegory. The Victorians, much to the chagrin of modernists like James, took very seriously what Michael McKeon has described as a "pedagogical end" of realism, that is, the teaching of precept by example.[2] George Eliot claims that she will not let her stories lapse "from the picture to the diagram," but the pedagogical end is absorbed into a decades-long parable that demonstrates, both in form and in subject matter, the ethical importance of telling the truth and of finding it out. These things, says George Eliot half-mockingly about the famous looking-glass metaphor in *Middlemarch*, are a "parable." Realism, then, even as it struggles out from the traditions that helped found it, is paradoxically an attenuated form of a distinctly non-realistic narrative practice.

Realism's giddying self-contradictory condition is confused yet further by the fact that it has one consistent commitment: the very hard work of trying to reach beyond words to describe the way things are. While, as I have argued, historical transformation of the culture's understanding of the way things are, and awareness of how different things look from different perspectives, makes realism apparently unstable, it manages to hold together just because it is always also committed to the commonsense notion that what we see – not our words or our ideas – is "really there," that the physical world is not a Cartesian dream but is really real, as opposed to being constituted of mere ideas or individual sensations. Realism is always committed to register the external real and then (or at the same time) the interiority that perceives it and distorts or penetrates it.

Despite much modern critical insistence, realism's effort to stand in for the world was not, among the great Victorian writers, naïve and self-deceived. Writing with a commitment to representing the real world adequately forces consideration of the extraordinary difficulties of the work of representation. It makes inevitable an intense self-consciousness, sometimes explicit, sometimes not. No writer attempting to reach beyond words can fail to be struck by the work words do, by the obstacles they put up to transparency, and therefore no such writer can fail to recognize the degree to which the creation of illusion is an essential feature of the realist process. Realism is an illusion, just as representational art is illusory, finding ways to suggest depth and three dimensions on a two dimensional canvas, finding strategies by which to create the sense of light, as the impressionists did, just by not making the brush strokes look like the thing being represented (except from certain viewing perspectives).[3]

While there certainly were many "realist" novels that seem simply to plunge in, tell their stories, describe their little (or not so little) worlds, and worry not at all about the nature of the perspective from which the story is to be told, or the problematic nature of the reality being described, on the whole realistic fiction is required to think about itself a great deal. That it does so is manifest in dozens of books that self-consciously announce to the reader that it won't be telling a romantic story, that it will labor hard at getting it right, and that, as George Eliot always conceded, the job was difficult and the "mirror" is never perfect.[4] Certainly, *Vanity Fair*, as we shall see, far from being casual about its representational strategies, is one of the most self-conscious books written in the period. If the world of the novel is to be represented as real (itself, of course, an oxymoronic condition), the first thing that has to be got straight is the difference between "reality," whatever we decide that is, and a work of literature, and the degree to which what is represented is being shaped by the author. That is to say, the realist novel has got to face the fact that it is a fiction, that it is made up – something that Thackeray does strenuously, if erratically, in *Vanity Fair*.

A line of Northrop Frye's economically summarizes the problem. "The realistic writer," Frye claims, "soon finds that the requirements of literary form and plausible content always fight against each other."[5] This is both self-evident and in some ways radically subversive of any pure realist enterprise – Biffin's, for example, in Gissing's *New Grub Street* (1891). His vast and ambitious work in progress, "Mr. Bailey, Grocer," will be, as Biffin himself knows, virtually unreadable, a record of everything in the life of "Mr. Bailey," an austere, endless representation of all the details of an ordinary life, the "ignobly decent," as he puts it. Biffin describes how he would, for example, represent the banal conversation between two lovers he hears in the street: "I am going to reproduce it verbatim without one single impertinent suggestion of any point of view save that of honest reporting. The result will be something unutterably tedious. Precisely. That is the stamp of the ignobly decent life. If it were anything but tedious it would be untrue" (ch. 10).

In a way, it is a cheat that Gissing finally allows Biffin actually to complete the manuscript – how could he ever have reached the end of these tedious registrations of the real? When Frye talks of the tension between literary form and plausibility, he is implying a fundamental tension in all realist texts, one that often manifests itself as a tension between focus on character and interest in plot. Biffin's realist novel will have no plot. Trollope distinguishes his own work from the "sensation novel," a subgenre in which the workings of plot and the discovery of how it will come out tend to create the driving energy. But for Trollope, the true work of the novel is "observation," and the true interest of the writer (and the readers) is in the characters. He argues that it should not matter if the reader knows the whole story. In reading a sensation novel (see chapter five), one is concerned to find out what will happen next, how the mysteries will be resolved, but reading a Trollopean, realist novel, one finds that the pleasure of the experience has little to do with the plot, which can seem an arbitrary authorial imposition on the narrative rather than intrinsic to the life and characters it is representing; the pleasure is just in the interest that develops in the representation of verisimilar objects and characters.

Although retrospectively it is easy to think of nineteenth-century realist fiction as sometimes plot heavy (not so, for the most part, with Trollope), it is characterized more significantly by a sort of "detailism" – intense observation of the particulars of the material world that the protagonists inhabit – and novels devoted to details, context, and character give less the illusion of manipulation than those in which what will happen is the driving force of the narrative. Insofar as the duality holds (and Trollope argues that it is artificial and that all novelists in the end must work at both poles), detailism and representation work toward plausibility and away from form, while plot works toward it. Thus, on the one hand, one has the "large, loose baggy monsters" of which James complains, and on the other, one has the stunning formal precision of *Wuthering Heights*, which meticulously organizes and balances events and sustains itself through the energies of romance. Nineteenth-century realism, as we can understand it today, leans toward the scrupulous construction of social and historical context, and to the life of characters within that context. In its fullest form, as Gissing imagines it in "Mr. Bailey, Grocer," it produces the most artless art, the least regardful of the requirements of literary form.

But this tendency of realism to formless and plotless representation of what can be observed and of character further compounds the paradoxes at the heart of the realist enterprise, for in order to write such a boring, realistic, heroless, plotless novel, Biffin must sustain the most austere, the most ascetic artistic commitment, giving his life to the writing of a book whose authenticity guarantees that it will be a commercial failure. Being a realist for Biffin entails the most scrupulous and careful artistry, and what Gissing's conception of Biffin and his book does is crystallize just that very special tension in Victorian fiction created by the need for the most austere artfulness in the creation of what will look just like "life." Victorian novels, even the most realistic of them, are usually highly crafted, though the craft may be of a very different kind from that which Henry James desired. Given the distinction between art and realist representation, narrators must remain alert, perhaps not to the potential tediousness of their work but to the difference between what they can narrate and what is out there to be narrated. Biffin could never, really, have finished that book just because Frye is right. The plausible has no beginning and no end.

Such problems of representation require that the realist novelist think, first of all, about the question of perspective. Although "free indirect discourse" has a pre-nineteenth century history, its great development in Jane Austen and George Eliot, in particular, is obviously the work of realistic fiction. By mid-century, writers were particularly aware of the inadequacy of strictly omniscient representation of "reality" – among other things, the danger of a voice too authoritative, too unBiffinlike in determining the readers' judgments and understanding. Serious writers could not help have doubts about the power of omniscience really to be omniscient, or of the novel to contain all that is out there to be represented. Free indirect discourse is an ingenious compromise between first person narration, whose limits and unreliability have been part of novelists' problems since *Pamela*, and full omniscience. And free indirect discourse has turned out to be the best mode by which an author can "disappear," and give the impression that what unfolds on the page simply happens without his (or her) intervention or help. On the other hand, it allows interiority without subjecting the reader to the full bias of the characters' desires and prejudices and without the falsity of representation of thought that comes marked by quotation marks, as though the mind works precisely in the rhetorically imposing way that stage representation requires. Moreover, free indirect style encourages the reader to be an active participant in the narrative rather than a passive receiver of "fact" and judgments, and thus further gives the sense that the narration is like life, in which there are no omniscient narrators to help us decide what to think about what we experience. The narrator is there, to be sure, in the third person perspective of passages of free indirect discourse, and a writer like George Eliot can occasionally interject an implicit judgment in the midst of such passages, as happens often with "poor Rosamond," or even "poor Dorothea," but characters whose consciousness is so recorded have the widest space in which to open themselves to the readers' judgments. Free indirect discourse is a remarkably devious invention in that it is extremely good at creating the illusion that consciousness is being rendered without authorial intervention, and that the language is the strictest representation, Biffinlike, of the workings of a real character's mind.

Omniscient narrations are far less illusory. If they are constrained by a single consciousness rather than revelatory of the free play of alternative voices, they still have the virtue of not fully disguising the presence of a narrator, and in realism, presumably, openness about the fact of the presence of a narrator makes a narration more "true," if, from the point of view of literary modernists, less artistically effective. There is a certain irony that Henry James, who was so self-consciously creating and theorizing the "art" of the novel, was so strongly committed to sustaining its illusions that he required the writer to delude readers into believing that they were in direct contact with the real. Consider how upset James gets at Trollope's habit of admitting he is writing a novel right in the middle of a novel – "He took a suicidal satisfaction in reminding the reader that the story he was telling was only, after all, a make-believe."[6] The worst sin a realist artist can commit, apparently, is to confess (truthfully and therefore realistically?) that he or she is making up a story.

Ironically, however, it is possible to think of the naïve Victorians as more sophisticated about novel theory than James himself, for the various ways in which they comment on their narratives has something of the postmodern about it. That is, they create their worlds while being intensely and often explicitly self-conscious about the medium through which they are doing it, and worrying not at all that the efforts at illusion will be undercut by overt exposures of the devices by which the illusion is being created. Who, among novel readers, does not know he or she is reading a novel? In the long run, it is not clear whether Jamesian modernism or Trollopean Victorianism is more "realistic," but it is also not clear which requires greater art.

II

There is no novel more self-conscious (and perhaps inconsistent) about the fact of its illusionism, about the difference between the claims of art and the claims of plausibility, about the inadequacies of omniscient representation in the efforts toward authentic representation of the real, than *Vanity Fair*. The narrator's representation of himself as a puppet master and of the characters as puppets is well known. But the narrator also appears as an "I" in the book, someone who, we are told quite late, has actually met Becky Sharp in Germany. If the characters are puppets, they are odd puppets, or it's an odd narrator; it becomes necessary, for any sort of consistency, to think of "puppets" as a metaphor, although, famously, there is a concluding vignette in which the "author" is in fact putting real puppets back in a box. Yet the narrator not only meets these puppets in Germany, but some of them provide him with information he needs to tell the story. Early on, in yet another guise, the narrator asks, "as a man and a brother," "to step down from the platform, and talk about" the characters he has been introducing (ch. 8). And in a move that might be recognized from Scott's *Waverley*, he pauses to tell "us" – and the "us," the readers, are very much part of the text – in what others ways "we might have treated this subject," and he goes on to describe other literary forms that he has, on consideration, rejected (ch. 6). In the role of omniscient narrator, he sometimes abdicates but then selectively loses his power to know everything, claiming that he is unable to tell us what have been the motives of his characters. If any narration can be taken to be unstable and inconsistent, the narration of *Vanity Fair* is it.

The inconsistency is both created and compounded by the fact that *Vanity Fair* is a persistently ironic book, far more so than *Pickwick Papers*. In the great Cervantean tradition, and in keeping with Thackeray's earlier work and the original title of the novel, "Pen and Pencil Sketches of English Society," *Vanity Fair* satirizes almost everything, using literary devices to counter literary devices, exploding conventional ways of writing a novel, even ending on a note that pulls the rug out from under any of us who, led by the conventions of comic romance, or comic realism, expect and wait hopefully for the marriage of Dobbin and Amelia. When that marriage comes, the possibilities of romance are long since gone, and even a touch of bitterness enters the prose:

> He has got the prize he has been trying for all his life. The bird has come in at last. There it is with its head on his shoulder, billing and cooing close up to his heart, with soft outstretched fluttering wings. This is what he has asked for every day and hour for eighteen years. This is what he pined after. Here it is – the summit, the end – the last page. (ch. 67, p. 804)[7]

The climax, then, arrives as the book announces (metaphorically) that it is a book and we are on the last page. As literature and life are conflated and comment on each other, the satire edges toward contempt, and its intensity raises the stakes. It is not only Amelia who makes an unsatisfactory bride, but marriage as an institution is implicated, and perhaps more seriously yet, the marriage plot itself is called into question, as well as the conventions of formal closure. Part of the irony of the passage is that just as it is announcing it has arrived at "the last page," it is developing the conventions that will dominate realism. That is, as I have already discussed it in relation to *Pickwick Papers*, it creates its reality by satirizing conventional literary form. The genre of realist fiction, which in England began and was sustained for the most part by the comic tradition that concludes the drama in marriage, increasingly tends to treat marriage not as an ending but as a beginning. Thackeray helps, boldly, to initiate this change: Becky marries Rawdon early on and the book explores many marriages with an ironic, one might almost say, embittered, tone. Twenty-five years later, George Eliot would make the very substance of perhaps the greatest English realist novel two marriages – that between Dorothea Brooke and Casaubon, which happens within a few chapters of the start of *Middlemarch*, and that between Rosamond and Lydgate, which happens not much later.

Thackeray's ironic comment on Amelia and Dobbin's marriage has large implications for the form of realist fiction, but it has also a biting ethical energy to it. It is not only a reaction to the obvious fact of the anguish of Thackeray's own marriage. It is angry more broadly about romantic illusion; it is angry about conventions of representation that take romantic love seriously. It is contemptuous of the happy ending, for it is clear that the requirements of literary form rub hard against the requirements of realistic representation as Thackeray understands the real. Any ending within a self-consciously realist text is going to be arbitrary; there can be no real conclusion. But Thackeray intimates this without allowing his book to answer to realism's potential shapelessness, for he uses the conventional ending even as he satirically employs it to undercut the convention.

The ending of *Vanity Fair* is, however, certainly an illusion. Becky Sharp, the "villainess" (who for many readers – significantly for the implications of Thackeray's book and for realism – is the real heroine of the book), lives outside the punishment that poetic justice would require, and despite the fact that there is a strong implication that she has murdered Amelia's brother. Her life goes on beyond "the last page." And another and different sort of novel begs to be written, Biffinlike, or perhaps Jameslike, exploring the interiority of a Dobbin who clearly no longer loves his wife but is gentle and good to her, and of an "Emmy" who knows this is the case. In refusing the satisfactions of closure, Thackeray is implicitly affirming the importance of the realist enterprise; in rejecting the comic ending and the possibility of a satisfactory conclusion ("Which of us is happy in this world?" the book's final paragraph asks), Thackeray is, with some fatigue, turning away from the literary forms that in fact give spine and structure to his own enormous book. Thackeray arrives at what might be seen as the ultimate attitude of the realist, something like contempt for the impossible enterprise and for the fantasies to which it aspires.

Vanity Fair is perhaps uncharacteristic of early Victorian fiction in that it is thick with disillusion, and yet that quality anticipates much that is central to the experience of realism. Insofar as the realist aspires to tell the truth, both author and reader must be perpetually disillusioned, for it is impossible not to be aware of limits to both transparency and comprehensiveness. Inclusion implies exclusion and "to take seriously any set of particulars is to falsify."[8] The focus on any character or set of characters, any object or set of objects, implies a denial of the importance of the characters or objects not described, but for Thackeray and the realists, implicitly, every object and every character is worthy of attention. A fully "realistic" novel would have to include everything with equal attention, and so there would be no focal figures; every figure would gather the fullest sympathetic and imaginative attention. There is, then, a moral implication to these kinds of exclusions, as, for example, when the narrator notes how doctors paid more attention to Amelia's son, Georgie, than to others: "did they sit up for the folks at the Pineries, when Ralph Plantagenet, and Gwendoline, and Guinever Mango had the same juvenile complaint? Did they sit up for little Mary Clapp, the landlord's daughter, who actually caught the disease off little Georgy?" (p. 451). Significantly, these "characters" appear nowhere else in the novel; they are other novels not written, of which the author, who will not write those novels, wants to remind us. As the narrator of *Middlemarch* forcefully does remind us, there are other sensibilities than that of our hero or heroine: "Why always Dorothea?" That is the realist question, thick with ethical implications, and it is a question that Thackeray is always asking.

Theme and form, in realism, play into each other – the questions of how much of reality can be represented, about whether reality can ever be represented at all, are thematized in *Vanity Fair* as they often arc in other realist texts. But virtually every page plays out, in one way or other, problems that characteristically emerged in nineteenth-century realist fictions – problems clearly related to what Franco Moretti describes, following Karl Mannheim, as the collapse of status society.[9] As I pointed out in the first chapter, formal changes in literary narrative were tied closely to the economic and social transformations that were changing the face of England through the eighteenth and ninetenth centuries. We can see in *Vanity Fair* that Thackeray is indeed worrying about what Michael McKeon has called "questions of virtue," for the book implies reconceptions of the most fundamental categories of being – of religion and individuality and selfhood and privacy and public life and education and class. Most critically, as Moretti suggests, "the world of work changes at an incredible and incessant pace,"[10] and it was hard to be a "realist" at the time without making the question of the protagonist's vocation critical to the drama. In a genre addressed to a new middle-class audience, the question was less "Whom will I marry?" than "What can I do?" "What can I do?" echoes remarkably among the protagonists of a large number of Victorian novels. Although Thackeray focuses in his novel on class distinctions and aspiration, and his is a world aspiring to the condition of aristocracy, much of the narrative depends on the fact that Becky Sharp must make a living. She tries to make it the old way for women, by marrying up, but she just misses and thus for hundreds of pages her story is devoted to her quest for money, a quest that leads to those two brilliant virtuoso chapters on "How to Live on Nothing a Year."

The other side of the question of vocation is the question of inheritance, which had a long life in pre-realist genres, and which oddly but significantly survives well into the history of nineteenth-century realism. Inheritance in Victorian novels is often the key to the crossing of classes, which is one of the central preoccupations of Victorian fiction. Becky counts on inheritance in the first half of the novel and worries about what "to do" only after it's clear that the inheritance will not come her way. Amelia spends much of the book living with the consequence of being disinherited. All of these issues are entangled with questions of class and vocation just because they are manifestations of the new instability of class status, as, in the reshuffling of the orders of power in nineteenth-century society, money and class came to be fundamentally separate categories, even while the fundamental attitudes of a hierarchical society remained in place.

It is no accident, again, that one of the founding novels of modern English realistic fiction, *Pamela*, whose heroine Fielding recreated as the maid-heroine Shamela, narrates through letters the story of a pre-Becky. But the narrative of crossing classes is also the narrative of "virtue rewarded," a phrase that has formal as well as ethical implications. Implicitly, the narrative of middle-class realist fiction will be one that issues finally in the rewarding of virtue, which means, in formal terms, comedy – the right woman marries the right man, and all discord and injustice are resolved in the comic ending.

All of these almost obsessive preoccupations of realist fiction, their relation to the ethical, their relation to the practice of accurate representation, and their relation, finally, to literary form, cause a fundamental crisis in realist practice. This crisis, which, I would argue, is a key force in realism's constant formal transformations – the place of marriage in the narratives, for example, or the shift to focus on characters' interiority, or the move away from comic to something like tragic form – is a peculiarly secular one. The problems with which the realist novel engages are, as the title "Vanity Fair" suggests, secular problems. The realist novel is predominantly a secular form, in which the implicit order of the world inferable from traditional comic and tragic and epic forms, can only be achieved in worldly terms. The achievements of traditional comic form depend on an implicit faith that justice and meaning are built into the world, and the imbalance and hierarchical nature of the social order could be justified by a sense of the reality of the transcendent and a world beyond. Virtue could be rewarded because virtue was rewarded in a just and divinely ordered world; success could go with comic conclusions because success was not contaminated by worldly corruptions. But almost all of this was slowly, inexorably changed and complicated by the development of new economic and social orders in which money was displacing class status as the chief mark of success, and in which money was increasingly conceivable apart from class status. Such a transformation could not help but have powerful effects on the nature of literary genres themselves, and could not help but be central to the Victorian novel, which self-consciously sought to represent the modern world and its rising middle class as they really were.

Conceiving a world in which money trumps class, in effect becoming class and making social status fluid, the Victorian realist novel, despite its tendency toward what might be called "providential plots," tried to rely exclusively on secular means rather than on interventions from above. The critical question for protagonists becomes how to get money, although that question is frequently displaced and disguised. The story of Fred Vincy in *Middlemarch* is a prime example, in encapsulated form, of the kind of problem with which realistic fiction persistently engaged. For Fred begins life assuming an inheritance that he does not get. One kind of life-narrative immediately transforms into another: what is it that Fred can do to earn the money he will need to survive and succeed (and win his beloved's hand)? *Middlemarch* makes the subject of his narrative, then, the question of work itself. And while in *Vanity Fair* we have no such focus on work, in fact Becky's story anticipates the pattern (though as a woman her story is somewhat different, and she seeks money through love relations).

Money becomes the pivot, implicit or explicit, on which nineteenth-century realist fiction turns. Certainly, whatever the ostensible issues, there can be no success in the world of Victorian realism without money, however disguised its sources are. As I suggested earlier, one of they key aspects of *Pickwick Papers* is Pickwick's money, about which the narrative never talks. Where did it come from? The refusal of money talk allows Pickwick to remain the innocent, which he simply could not have been had we been told how he acquired the money. *Pickwick* hovers between comic myth and realism just because it glances so lightly over things that a straightforwardly realist narrative could not afford to ignore. Money, of course, is everywhere in *Vanity Fair*, even when the characters are without it. Absence of money is the fundamental fact of Amelia's story after the death of George, and all the pathos and tensions of that story depend on money's absence. But when the question of virtue is tied to the question of money, the realist novel is faced with ethical (and formal) problems that it often tries to evade. It is one of the ironies of English nineteenth-century realism that while money is essential for success, and therefore for the comic ending, the quest for money (beyond what is necessary for survival, and sometimes even then) is unequivocally a mark of shame, corruption, evil. Anthony Trollope makes one of the major exceptions to this generalization. The essential question, often not articulated, is how it can be possible for a protagonist to sustain the moral virtues that the culture admires and at the same time achieve success. The realist novel is persistently driven to imagine such figures, and with very mixed results.

The concepts of intrinsic virtue and of some ultimate possibility of moral justice depend on the sense that moral order is built into the world and that, in the long run, worldly troubles are compensated for in the light of divine oversight and presence. The world, otherwise, is both an ethical and aesthetic catastrophe, rather like what John Henry Newman believed the world without God to be:

> To consider the world in its length and breadth, its various history, the many races of man, their starts, their fortunes, their mutual alienation, their conflicts; and then their ways, habits, governments, forms of worship; their enterprises, their aimless courses, their random achievements and acquirements, the impotent conclusion of long-standing fact, the tokens so faint and broken of a superintending design, the blind evolution of what turn out to be great powers or truths, the progress of things, as if from unreasoning elements, hot towards final causes, the greatness and littleness of man, his far-reaching aims, his short duration, the curtain hung over his futurity, the disappointments of life, the defeat of good, the success of evil, physical pain, mental anguish, the prevalence and intensity of sin, the pervading idolatries, the corruptions, the dreary hopeless irreligion, that condition of the whole race, so fearfully yet exactly described in the Apostle's words, "having no hope and without God in the world," – all this is a vision to dizzy and appall; and inflicts upon the mind the sense of a profound mystery which is absolutely beyond human solution.

What Newman describes in this exhausting, breathtaking catalogue of the conditions of this world is Vanity Fair itself – a vision to dizzy and appall. Many Victorian realists, most brilliantly and strenuously George Eliot, tried to imagine into the secular world the sort of moral order that Newman here describes as impossible. Thackeray's response to this horrific vision is to make comedy and satire but, beyond that, to leave each of us corrupted and, as the narrator concludes, unsatisfied.

Vanity Fair is a good representative of nineteenth-century realism just because it so doggedly insists on confining its narration to the doings of "Vanity Fair." While the very determination to do that and to invoke Bunyan's place can reasonably enough suggest the possibility of a divine if hidden presence in the world or at least of a genuine piety, Thackeray's novel treats religion as it treats commercial culture – it is simply a fact of this lower world and plays into the narrative as it affects such things as inheritance. Certainly, the book's clergy are totally worldly figures. Its preoccupations, however, with class, with commercial success, with social climbing, with "how to live on nothing a year," with hypocrisy, and with inheritance are secular to the extreme. The narrator closes the door on Amelia's prayers because, he claims, these are not the province of Vanity Fair, but it would be no stretch to suggest that Thackeray himself closed off a representation of that kind of piety just because it would change the nature of the novel itself (and perhaps might be merely sentimentally tedious).

III

A comment of Becky Sharp's will help focus the problems of realism discussed here. In chapter 41, she pauses to reflect as she rises toward the high point of her career, just before her audience with the king himself, and she thinks about the way in which the entirely virtuous Lady Jane, having inherited a large sum of money, conducts herself. "I think," thinks Becky, "I could be a good woman if I had five thousand a year." The omnipresent, though rather elusive narrator then comments: "And who knows but Rebecca was right in her speculations – and that it was only a question of money and fortune which made the difference between her and an honest woman."

This seems innocuous enough, just a little piece of Becky's cynicism and a little piece of Thackeray's irony. But Becky's comment might, if taken in another way, represent a fundamental conflict in realism's conception of character and of its relation to the scrupulously detailed and historically precise world in which characters in realist fiction move. And the narrator's comment might, ironically, be taken as quite literal.

So there is a double irony here. The first is the narrator's commentary on Becky's reflection, which seems to imply that qualities of character do not depend on circumstance. But the more telling irony is that the narrator's ironies might not be ironic at all. Realist practice, throughout its literary life, is to insist on the context in which characters move, on the details I've mentioned before, on history, on social context. That supertext of realism, *Middlemarch*, for example, is subtitled *A Study of Provincial Life*. Here the question of secularity looms large, for realism is the mode that reads character into the conditions of ordinary life, the life of Vanity Fair, and makes drama of their apparent everydayness, of their problems in making a living, of their relations with their neighbors, of the things that they have and want, of their domesticity. Every character in a realist novel must be read in relation to the circumstances of his or her life, and whatever we make of Becky's speculation, this is almost universally true of the characters in *Vanity Fair*.

Vanity Fair makes much of what happens in the story dependent on the great historical moment of Waterloo and the defeat of Napoleon – Amelia's father loses his fortune because of the war; Amelia loses her husband in it; and the book is careful to test the quality of its major characters against the event, without ever directly representing it (a world-historical event and therefore beyond the borders of a domestic realist narrative). Becky emerges from Waterloo as something of a Napoleonic figure, but it is also clear from earlier information we get about her that who Becky is depends partly on where she comes from, who her parents were, what class she belongs to, what possibilities are open to a young woman without wealth, and of course what is going on in Europe at the time she comes of age. Part of what evoked disgust from many readers of *Vanity Fair* was just the cynical sense it intimated (even while resisting it with ambiguous ironies) that Becky is at least partly right and the narrator is not being ironic.

Even if we are to take the narrator's comment as ironic, aware that the novel shares the cultural revulsion from the idea that character is not integrally and permanently itself, that it is not either intrinsically virtuous or intrinsically evil, and that money can be determining even of goodness, Thackeray's way of handling the issues, of observing as a good realist should, raises questions. His narrative reveals what he may be ironically disparaging in his comment on Becky's thought. Becky's way of thinking about virtue, which many readers did in fact take as Thackeray's, made the book morally repellent, even disgusting, to many. On the other hand, when George Eliot made pretty much the same point in another way and as a central theme of her novels, she was, by and large, taken with the greatest seriousness and respect. One of the most famous lines in all of George Eliot's novels comes near the end of *Middlemarch*, when she asserts, "For there is no creature whose inward being is so strong that it is not greatly determined by what lies outside it" ("Finale," p. 821).[11] But this is what Becky was saying, if in a less solemn, less personal mode! The fact that George Eliot's novels, like a large proportion of realist novels, have no intrinsically evil people in them (except perhaps Grandcourt in *Daniel Deronda* [1876]) is a reflection of this sense of character. Mr. Farebrother, the gentle and generous clergyman in *Middlemarch*, tells Dorothea: "character is not cut in marble – it is not something solid and unalterable. It is something living and changing, and may become diseased as our bodies do" (ch. 72, p. 724). The bad guys in George Eliot's fiction, like Tito Melema in *Romola* (1863), or even Arthur Donnithorne in *Adam Bede*, go bad because of circumstance, or at least partly because of circumstance. It is true that realism, as it is manifested in Thackeray and George Eliot, tends to hold on for a long time to a sense of an intrinsic self that may be pushed and strained by circumstance but that is nevertheless whole and integral. But all strong realists understand that circumstance can become decisive. And thus Becky's reflections, which ought to be further evidence of her corruption and the shallowness of her moral sense, take on great significance for realist texts, including *Vanity Fair*. She writes like a novelist in many parts of the book, and here she is even thinking like a novelist – a realist, secular one.

Nor is it an accident that Becky's reflections take us back to the question of money. Whatever the intentions of the writers, in the realist tradition money is usually a determining, even a decisive factor both for the form of the book and for the fate of the characters. Becky acknowledges (and has always acknowledged) to herself what the society won't admit, that virtue is somehow closely tied to money, and that money is the key element in the secular world. The focus on money, in fact, is the firmest mark that realist fiction is fundamentally secular. The fluidity of class identity, as I have suggested, is represented in Victorian realist novels by the new fluidity of money. Money's power to corrupt corresponds, in a way, to the vision of the material world that Newman describes. It displaces an ordering god, for it is the condition of success, the condition of the happy ending. The difference is that many Victorian realist novels either avoid confronting the ways in which money works to build success, or exonerate its protagonists from concern for money by allowing them to inherit it (and thus not dirty their hands in its acquisition), simply to have it all along, or to show along the way that although they have it, they really don't care for it and would never compromise themselves to retain it.

A roll call of representative Victorian novels will make clear how broadly this argument applies. Even Jane Eyre inherits out of the blue the money that gives her the power to save Rochester and to aid her cousins, and she gives away most of it. Pip, in *Great Expectations*, who has been corrupted by money, can only be redeemed by risking all of it, losing all of it, in order to save the life of his benefactor; Margaret in *North and South* (1855) inherits the money that she wants to give to Thornton, and their declaration of love is in fact based on her renunciation of her money for him; Little Dorrit achieves happiness only because she is bankrupt, and Clennam can accept her for the same reason. The heroes of Victorian novels are notoriously weak and ineffectual largely because strong heroes would have to be shown in the capitalist game of successful pursuit of money, where Scroogelike figures are more likely to be in control. Becky Sharp might have been portrayed as another kind of heroine, someone who having led a difficult and penurious childhood struggles up to success, say, like Jane Eyre. But Becky is allowed to be seen pursuing money, and in the shadiest of ways, and that pursuit marks her as the wicked mermaid, the "monster" whose "hideous tail" flaps invisibly under water. Against Becky's betrayal of Rawdon as she milks Lord Steyne of everything she gets, the novel juxtaposes Amelia's solitary struggle for money enough to give little Georgie the most elementary things. The absence of money forces her to give up Georgie to his grandfather, Mr. Osborne. For both women, money is the critical need but the juxtaposition sets up the limits of what relation to money is morally sustainable.

The work of the realist, to represent things as they are, and in this case the workings of an economy that is ruthless and selfish, the secular order in which money is the essential condition both for survival and for power, leads to a recognition, built into the very title of Thackeray's novel, that things as they are do not include the moral and just distribution of rewards. Vanity Fair does not allow very often for the form of comedy (except as comedy is structured around ironies), does not provide those resolutions in union and community that are normally marked by marriage and the marriage plot, but perhaps most important, does not allow active people to avoid the contamination and even corruption that engagement with the economic order entails. Hapless and affectionate as Amelia is, her sentimental passion for Georgie, as it causes strains with her mother and father, is itself morally strained. That most early nineteenth-century realist texts tend to end with marriages, the clearest form of the distribution of justice possible, often strains the commitment to probability that is part of the realist project. That *Vanity Fair* in effect mocks this tradition makes part of its power as a representative of the realist impulse. Unlike, say, *Villette* (1853), in which Lucy and M. Paul do come together, if even for a very brief moment, *Vanity Fair* allows for no happy marriages: Becky and Rawdon, Amelia and George, Amelia and Dobbin provide, in the end, no sense of justice or order.

But in the 1840s *Vanity Fair* was unusual. If David Copperfield's first marriage was inadequate, the second, with Agnes pointing upward, was just right for a comic ending. Adam Bede and Dinah finally come together despite Adam's mistaken fascination with Hetty Sorrel. These endings suggest an ultimate meaningfulness in a secular world that seems marked by Newmanian disorder and meaninglessness, and for the most part, in the comic tradition of early nineteenth-century realism, the world, though threatening, does not get malicious, or indifferent.

It is a commonplace of modern reception of Victorian fiction that it is marked by often extravagant and barely plausible coincidence. Isn't it a remarkable coincidence that Jane Eyre, on the verge of death, stumbles upon the house of cousins? Isn't it a coincidence that Casaubon in *Middlemarch* dies just at the point at which Dorothea was preparing to throw away her life for him; isn't it a coincidence that Margaret Hale inherits money from her father's friend in time for her to save Thornton's factory? Isn't it a coincidence that Little Dorrit loses her money just in time to save Clennam? Isn't it a coincidence that Lucy Snowe is rescued in *Villette* by the family that first took her in in England? Isn't it a coincidence that Daniel Deronda turns out to be Jewish after all, and thus can satisfy both his future wife, Mirah, and her messianic brother?

Vanity Fair, on the other hand, doesn't rely on coincidences. And this is, I would argue, because the book is so doggedly determined to see the secular world as Newman sees it. It doesn't make sense. It doesn't satisfy. Coincidence can be the instrument of the providential plot, and without providence coincidence is simply implausible. The struggle of the secular novelist to build comic plots depends upon an assumption that the world intrinsically does make sense, but without God to provide the meaning missing from strictly secular conditions. Thus, most of the early Victorians tend to intimate a religious order somewhere behind the disorder of the world, as Dickens did most famously in the religious imagery of *Little Dorrit*. Coincidence functions rather like the *Deus ex machina* of early literary forms, but gods are not allowed.

This order increasingly breaks down as realist fiction continues to explore the possibilities available to the ignobly decent, as Biffin would have it, in an intensely competitive society. One way I have found to read the tensions that this struggle produced for the very form of Victorian fiction is through the lens of Max Weber's theory laid out in *The Protestant Ethic and the "Spirit" of Capitalism* (1905). A significant proportion of English nineteenth-century novels test out Weber's thesis that the ascetic virtues that Calvinist religion required turn out to be precisely the virtues that are required for success in a capitalist economy. One of the central features of the "Protestant spirit" that Weber discusses is just that it shares the Victorian novel's distrust of money. Ironically, the Protestant spirit is financially successful in large part because practicing Calvinists did not work to get money, to acquire luxury, to make their lives easier, but because work and self-sacrifice were intrinsic to the Protestant calling. "Work while it is day," says Carlyle, referring to John 9:4, "for the night cometh in which no man can work." So, in a Weberian narrative, the most successful capitalist would turn out to be like the protagonists of Victorian novels, that is, uninterested in money, perhaps contemptuous of it, but interested in the work itself. Success and virtue would be two faces of the same coin.

George Eliot makes a gesture at this way of thinking about "success" in the character of Caleb Garth, in *Middlemarch*. Caleb is a capable and generous man who loves his work but cares not at all for money and is distrustful of those who pursue it. He makes of the word "business" an almost sacred icon just because it has nothing to do with money, as he understands it. And he makes a great success of his work. In his life, at least, virtue and secular success come together, and he is clearly to be read as a model. But it is no accident that his work is, in effect, pre-capitalist. More important, Caleb's story is almost a sidebar in a novel that carefully plots the failure of piety, and even of talent, because of the pull of money. The true ascetic, the true pious Protestant who rules with a kind of moral despotism over Middlemarch, is Bulstrode, whom Caleb distrusts, and who is successful in a Weberian way, but who it turns out is absolutely corrupt. The story of Bulstrode beautifully exemplifies the problem, for while people do not know where he got his money in the first place, he can reign as the pious and wealthy and dominating banker. But when the source of his money is revealed it is shown to be incompatible with the piety he displays and insists on. Realist novels in effect test Weber's thesis and in forcing a detailed attention to the lives and methods of its central characters, consistently dramatize the incompatibility between true piety, requiring self-denial, and worldly success. The novels do not find a way to reconcile virtue and successful work in the new economy, and Dickens famously explores and elaborates this polarity, as in the character of Wemmick, in *Great Expectations*, who is in effect two different people, the inhumane man who works for Jaggers, and the loving son who makes his home his castle. These tests of characters' engagement with money and power make it increasingly difficult for the realist novel to sustain the comic form it held onto so long in England (while in Europe, for the most part, this kind of tension is not important because continental realism had no Victorian commitment to the providential plot and the happy ending).

Although reconciliation was for the most part impossible, there are plenty of realist novels that try it. Dinah Mulock Craik tries it in *John Halifax, Gentleman* (1856), taking for her protagonist a rags to riches hero who is utterly perfect both as a worker and as a man. It is an unusual book among the Victorians because it not only attempts to portray an active and a good man, but takes the risk of describing, at least a little, the nature of the work that earns him success. The more a realist novel delves into the details of money matters, the less successful it is in representing wholly or largely virtuous protagonists. "There is something almost awful in the thought of a writer undertaking to give a detailed picture of the actions of a perfectly virtuous being," says Henry James of *John Halifax*. "If Miss Mulock had weighed her task more fairly, she would have shrunk from it in dismay."[12] Other Victorian writers struggled with the problem. Few dared to invent such a character as Halifax, but largely, I think, because moral perfection in characters is incompatible with the realist project of finding subject and form in the ordinary. Realism, as *Vanity Fair* makes abundantly clear, keeps the world-historical and the truly heroic offstage; it is a world in which everyone is compromised in one way or other, as realist writers consistently took compromise to be the condition of normal existence. Thus the attempt to reconcile the Protestant spirit to capitalism, which on Weber's account was actually accomplished historically, has a very hard time of it in the world of realist narrative, when characters are forced to face the moral consequences of each of their choices and readers expect satisfying closure.

Realism's movement in late Victorian fiction from comic to tragic form later in the century is then only partly the result of the influence of French realism on the English. It is an almost inevitable consequence of a fundamentally secular reading of the world in which, inescapably, money becomes the condition for protagonists' success. Hardy, for example, was hostile to naturalism, but wrote novel after novel in which the ingredients of class struggle and the problem of work figured as importantly as in earlier Victorian novels. But in not a single novel (with the qualified exception of *Far From the Madding Crowd* [1874]) does he represent a strong male figure who manages to remain both successful and virtuous. The world of Victorian realism turns upside down in Hardy as he self-consciously imagines his characters in a world that is so totally secular that it almost becomes, at times, demonic. "The President of the Immortals," for example, presides over the fate of Tess of the D'Urbervilles (1891), so that even at this late date in the history of nineteenth-century realism the ironic tradition in realism is at work, and the doubleness of its implications remains. Rejecting the possibility of the transcendent and of the ideal – in fact, plotting his stories, like that of Angel Clare, around the disastrous consequences of attempting to live the ideal – Hardy keeps the very literary and ideal qualities of realism alive. Tess is after all a "pure woman," and the President of the Immortals is a modern version of God.

Realism, throughout its Victorian history, remained an ambivalent and often self-contradictory mode. It was consistent only in its determination to find strategies for describing the world as it was, and inconsistent, of course, if only because every artist's conception of what the world was differed and the world changed from moment to moment, generation to generation. But it consistently worried ethical issues around the developments in contemporary economy and society, and so it regularly failed to find a satisfying way to represent an active and virtuous protagonist who achieves success without being corrupted along the way. It struggled to reconcile success and virtue, but was too honest as a literary mode to accomplish that easily. Its commitment to close observation of the details of society and the context in which characters move helped destabilize the conception of selfhood and character on which the Victorian novel built its greatest successes. Through Victorian realism the strategies of dramatizing and investigating individual consciousness were developed brilliantly into free indirect discourse, climaxing in the work of Henry James (an American Victorian, perhaps). In the world of realism, as in the world that Darwin was representing to his culture, everything is in flux, including character.

Thackeray's *Vanity Fair* is most interesting in its anticipatory exploration of realism's problems, problems both ethical and aesthetic, problems of perspective, of narrative voice, of characterization, and of the consequences of the relation between character and context. What contemporary readers found disgusting and disturbing about its worldliness are some of its most interesting virtues: its concession that we are all compromised and partly corrupted by money, its implication that behind the secular world there is no force for order and justice, its refusal of the happy ending because it will not reconcile success and merit (or not quite), its delicious indulgence in the things of this world, and its cynicism that powers its satire.

Reconciling probability and literary form in a world gone secular was ultimately the greatest challenge to the Victorian realist sensibility, most pressingly because Victorian novelists felt themselves committed to helping the new middle class understand itself, come to terms with its new status, and adhere closely to religious and moral conditions that sometimes made Victorian novels seem like handbooks to the good middle-class life. Hardy, resisting the label of naturalist or realist, argued that his books were not at all "reality," but pursuits of the design in the carpet. In the ambiguous status of Victorian realism, it should be enough to say that it remained throughout its long career a very literary mode, one that, even in its modern incarnations, often tries to disguise its literariness and one that must remain partial in its representations, and therefore vulnerable to the kinds of critiques I invoked at the start of this chapter. But it is a mode that by virtue of its commitment to getting it right and its passionate pursuit of honesty is in constant flux, changing its conception of the real with the movement of time, reimagining character and even selfhood – in an enterprise in which Becky herself participates – both in the context of the social conditions in which it must live and through the kinds of experiments with interiority that mark its history from Austen, to George Eliot, to James, on into the twentieth century. Its very weaknesses – its failure, for example, to imagine strong male protagonists, or its tendency not to consider the details by which protagonists do make money and achieve power, its exploitation of coincidences to achieve what a thorough pursuit of probability could not – these and others are also marks of its remarkable aspirations and indications of its extraordinary achievements, as well.

Notes

1   J. Hillis Miller, "Narrative and History," *ELH*, 41 (1974): 455–73; "Optic and Semiotic in *Middlemarch*," in *The Worlds of Victorian Fiction*, ed. J. H. Buckley (Cambridge, MA: Harvard University Press, 1975); "The Fiction of Realism: *Sketches by Boz, Oliver Twist*, and Cruikshank's Illustrations," in *Dickens Centennial Essays*, ed. Ada Nisbet and Blake Nevius (Berkeley: University of California Press, 1971), pp. 85–153.

2   See Michael McKeon, *Theory of the Novel: A Historical Approach* (Baltimore: Johns Hopkins University Press, 2000), p. 610.

3   See Elizabeth Deeds Ermarth, *Realism and Consensus in the English Novel* (Princeton: Princeton University Press, 1983). Ermarth discusses at great length the development of perspective in European art and shows, among other things, how "realism" is built not on naïve assumptions about how reality can be directly represented, but by cultural consensus.

4   For a discussion of this convention with examples, see George Levine, *The Realistic Imagination: The English Novel from Frankenstein to Lady Chatterley* (Chicago: University of Chicago Press, 1981).

5   Northrop Frye, *Fables of Identity: Studies in Poetic Mythology* (New York: Harcourt, Brace, 1963), p. 36.

6   Henry James, "Anthony Trollope," *Essays on Literature; American Writers; English Writers* (New York: Library of America, 1984), p. 1343.

7   *Vanity Fair* (London: Penguin Books, 2001).

8   George Levine, *The Realistic Imagination: English Fiction from Frankenstein to Lady Chatterley* (Chicago: University of Chicago Press, 1981), p. 154.

9   For an indispensable discussion of the *Bildungsroman* as the characteristic form of the early nineteenth century, see Franco Moretti, *The Way of the World: The Bildungsroman in European Culture* (London: Verso, 1987), p. 4 and *passim*. The *Bildungsroman* is perhaps the most important subgenre of realist fiction. In describing the ways in which "youth" is reconceived and redramatized, particularly in relation to work, Moretti provides an excellent overview of the nature of English realism as well.

10   Moretti, *The Way of the World*, p. 4.

11   *Middlemarch* (Oxford: Oxford University Press, 1996).

12   James, *Essays on Literature*, p. 845.

Chapter 4

Jane, David, and the *Bildungsroman*

I

As indicated in earlier chapters, the dominance of realism as a literary mode coincided with the great economic and social transformations that went into the creation of a literate middle class. These developments were accompanied by the efflorescence of the form that most centrally characterizes those transformations, and gives fullest expression to the concerns, desires, and ideals of the new middle class – the *Bildungsroman*. We take for granted now that novels might trace the lives of seemingly ordinary protagonists from early childhood, or, at least, that narratives might build around the movement to maturity of young people whose innocence and vulnerability and misguided ambitions and idealism lead them into troubles that it takes several hundred pages to resolve. But there is nothing inevitable about this kind of subject, and it was in the nineteenth century, and particularly among the Victorians, that it became central.[1]

Although only a small proportion of Victorian novels can, strictly speaking, be called *Bildungsromane*, it is striking how many novels, even the famous sensation novels like Wilkie Collins' *The Moonstone* (1868) and *The Woman in White* (1860), trace the maturing of young people usually either orphaned, or without a father or effective parents. The young, who are the protagonists of all *Bildungsromane*, become in that form the perfect embodiments of the movement from one social and economic order to another; usually, these characters mark the transition geographically, moving from the country to the city; in effect, they enact the kinds of transitions that were marking the whole of society, so that the *Bildungsroman* as a form sustains a sense of deeply personal, private, and highly interiorized individuality while at the same time it feels entirely representative. It was a form that was effectively born in the eighteenth century with Goethe's *Wilhelm Meister*, and it is no mere historical or personal accident that that book was translated by the first of the great Victorian sages, Thomas Carlyle, long before he became a "sage." It invites us to see the world through the initially innocent eyes of a young person, to sympathize with him (or her) in his mistakes as he enters a complicated new social order, and to rejoice in the successes achieved through maturity; it describes a career that can only have been experienced in a society converting from a traditional to a more modern, urban, and indeed capitalist mode.

The lives of most *Bildung* protagonists are childish in the sense that they are, at least at the start of their careers, open and absorptive and impressionable. The innocent vision of the child is privileged, while at the same time it is shown to be inadequate to the new world in which the child must grow and make his way. While the inheritance plot is hard to avoid in Victorian novels, the fates of the protagonists are largely shaped by what they do, by their intrinsic capacity to deal with the conflicting and potentially corrupting experiences with which they engage. Their fates are not, by and large, determined by tradition or by initial social status, although the moral crises into which their engagement with modernity thrusts them frequently require saving interventions, which also frequently means inheritance after all. Much of their lives is in fact given over to resisting the traditional but in the end coming to terms with it. It is striking how many such narratives flirt with "inheritance," but leave the protagonist more or less disinherited.

That is the key to the plot of *Great Expectations*, in which Pip redeems himself by attempting to save his benefactor even at the cost of all his unearned wealth. It is the story of Fred Vincy in *Middlemarch*, whose life spins on his being disinherited near the start of the novel. For women protagonists, there are parallel but usually distinctly different patterns of development – as for Jane Eyre, who does get a small inheritance, and for Margaret Hale, in *North and South*, whose unexpected inheritance makes the happy ending possible.[2] But in every case, male or female, it is not what one is, by rank and inheritance, but what one does that finally determines both personal value and worldly success, and the novels dramatize the process of education (of personal formation) that determines finally what the protagonists "do."

The *Bildung* narrative in Victorian novels thus traces the growth to mature consciousness of an individual who, without parents, though sometimes with inadequate foster parents (sisters, uncles, cousins), develops a powerful internal life that is imaginatively well beyond the constraining realities of actual life. By exercise of will and through consciousness of those realities, the protagonist learns to move upward (usually by way of transfer to the city) in the social scale and, at the same time, to achieve the kind of maturity that allows rejection of romantic ambitions and requires accommodation, by way of moral strength, to the compromised but ethically justified and moderate world of the realistic imagination. The central drama of these novels of education (the original meaning of the word *Bildung*), of development, of "formation," revolves around how romantic, childish illusions are cleared away, and around the consequences of the disenchantment – does it lead to a new maturity? To a shattering disillusion? These novels are written as though, as Franco Moretti has said, youth is "the most meaningful part of life."[3] Before Freud, that is, the Victorian novelists knew that the experiences of childhood are profoundly formative and require the sorts of consideration normally given to adult experience.

The easy strangeness of so much Victorian fiction has much to do with our contemporary assumptions about the importance of childhood and what is really our quite Victorian sense of how attractive, sympathetic, and complicated children are. The Victorians, rather than stodgy upholders of conventional moral restraints, were – in their very worries about the dangers of moral unrestraint – part of a grand revolution of sensibility going on in both art and society, a revolution that was partly a consequence of those profound economic and social changes that disrupted the bases of power and wealth in the country. The novel, though never really a strict record and representation of the way things are, became the register of the transformation, but most particularly of the way those whose lives had been shaped by that transformation thought about and valued it. Childhood, it has often been said, was invented by the romantics, and just as realism broke with traditions of what sorts of protagonists deserved focal attention, so it broke with the tradition that kept children always in the background of major narratives. They were not, the Victorians insisted and dramatized, merely small adults. The Victorian novelists, the realists too, were inheritors of romanticism and its new regard for childhood – the child is, indeed, father to the man.

We meet Pip in *Great Expectations*, an orphan if ever there was one, chilled and frightened in the marshes – a scene that gives a child's unidentifiable fears a powerful presence in the mature reader's consciousness. But Pip follows the direction of his *Bildung* compatriots up and out of

childish imagination and provincial roots. He moves from virtual appren-
ticeship to a country blacksmith, by way of several misunderstandings
and money given to him by a criminal, to the upper reaches of the urban
middle class, only to fall back into the very middle middle-classness of the
white collar worker, but not – it should be noted – into the condition of
a blacksmith. There is no returning to that pre-capitalist innocence, but
Pip's rejection of the great wealth available to him becomes, in the crisis of
the novel, the triumph of ethics and love over the apparently insuperable
power of "capital." Although the narrative crushes romantic and excessive
ambition – as narratives from *Don Quixote* forward have tended to do
– the story still embodies that aspiration upwards, the possibility of
"upward mobility," that is the mark of the new society. It makes drama
out of the personal moral and psychological tensions that accompany social
change, and in a way becomes a kind of exemplary tale, both confirming the ambition upon which capitalist society depends and rejecting
"unrealistic" ambition.

Pip begins without enough of the Protestant ethic, but by way of what
might be thought of as undeserved inheritance he achieves a level of
worldly success anyway. But integrity and the other virtues of the Protestant ethic in fact work against Weber's thesis that the Protestant virtues do
lead to worldly success. While Weber's thesis may well hold out in the real
world of Victorian society, the novelists, and Dickens in particular, are too
alert to the compromises and deceits entailed in the daily practice of business in the man's world of the new urban society to allow their protagonists to enter that world unequivocally. The Protestant ethic does not
work in *Great Expectations*, as it does not work in most Victorian novels,
to produce worldly success. Ambition for worldly success is almost universally corrupt in the novel, so that *Great Expectations* enacts the fundamental ambivalence of Victorian attitudes towards modernity. There is
Joe, the simple and loving blacksmith, the true practitioner of the Protestant ethic, who serves as a moral model and is a major cause of Pip's great
and unfocused guilt, but who is absolutely incapable of moving successfully in the new economic order; and there is Jaggers, who exploits the
guilt and criminality that is central to urban life and capitalist economics
and become a figure of enormous – almost mysterious – power as a result.

The richness of Dickens' famous novel makes any focus on its "moral"
reductive. Literature is never simply a replication of reality, nor is it
a sermon. It is a creative imagination of its subject that can at once
attempt to reproduce faithfully and to create – as Wordsworth had put

it, half-perceive and half-create. Pip's adventures resonate with the tensions that seem to have marked mid-nineteenth century urban life, and at the same time impose on that reality a creative vision that is at once singular and full of a broad common appeal. In its taming of ambition and romantic fantasy it implies the inadequacy of the higher social order to which Pip aspires (and about which, undoubtedly, Dickens himself felt ambivalent); it relentlessly exposes its duplicity and competitive ruthlessness; and against these Dickens explores the possibility of redemption from its worst qualities by way of the assertion of non-Jaggersian, non-utilitarian value.

When in that famous opening scene, Pip is turned upside down by the apparently monstrous convict, and the steeple appears under Pip's feet, we can get something of the feeling of freshness and strangeness generated by these narratives of children maturing over hundreds of pages. Dickens surely had nothing of the sort in mind, but that image can be taken to imply the social and even religious transformations with which the *Bildung* narrative inevitably engaged. Focusing as it does on the world as perceived by young Pip, it can be understood as dramatizing the centrality of individual consciousness to the new way of seeing the world that these narratives implied, and the "naturalness" of the childish vision, which, in its very childishness, has an unambivalent relation to reality. It is impossible to confront those early pages of the novel without a sympathetic leap inside the child's mind, without sharing the child's vision. Forced inside that child's consciousness, readers can hardly resist recognizing how powerful and important childhood experience is, and beyond that, how outside the moral and social norms it must be. That brutal education at nasty schools figures so frequently in Victorian novels – for example, *Nicholas Nickleby* (1839), *Jane Eyre* (1848), *David Copperfield* (1850) – further suggests that the literal application of moral norms to vulnerable and deep feeling children amounts to cruelty, not education.

What we take for granted as a norm and what we perceive as a regular component of Victorian fiction was, then, being constructed by the novelists. For them, childhood and youth are not only formative, but intrinsically intense and valuable moments. What has often since the years of early modernism been taken as merely sentimental concern with childhood was in the nineteenth century the major manifestation of the Romantic revolution – both psychological and social. It is ironic then that the English realist novel's focus on childhood, while it tended to dramatize and affirm the instability of traditional social order, sought also a replacement for that destabilized past, and thus became, in its turn, somewhat conservative itself. Current criticism, even the very best of it, has insisted on the conservative force of the Victorian *Bildungsroman*.[4] So Pip's willingness to sacrifice all his money in an attempt to hide and rescue his criminal benefactor affirms a kind of moral order that would resist the tendencies of capitalism to push relentlessly toward greater acquisition and to make "money" its exclusive value. In one reading, this makes *Great Expectations* not so much an attack on utilitarian value and the inhumane elements of capitalism, but a defense of a culture in which what the novels suggest are wicked aspects of this new social order can be overcome by virtuous acts of will. So despite the obvious attacks on the inhumane system that, for example, forces Wemmick to split himself in two, half family man, half inhuman mechanism with a post office slot for a mouth, the books are taken to imply that it is not the system itself that is at fault. Wemmick might be viewed as outside of the system when he is in his "castle" of a home. But surely Dickens also recognized that the privacy of the home is part of the very system that produces the inhumanity of Wemmick's post-office-box mouth.

There is a further irony that cannot be pursued at length here, but the traditional values of family, loyalty, and love – values that Joe may be said to represent – are wickedly satirized at the start of the novel in the portrait of Pip's sister and Pumblechook and others of the town, particularly at the interrupted Christmas dinner. But Joe's virtues remain unquestioned and Pip's discomfort with them gives substance to the implicit moral claim that these traditional values seem to make in the book. It is these values, exactly not the values of urban capitalist society, that constrain and also enrich individual lives as they are thrust into the life of the city. The claims of loyalty, in the end, are to override the claims of money.

But money keeps talking in Victorian fiction, and often in a very loud voice, even when – in particular when – its important presence is undiscussed. Pip's upward mobility depends upon money. At the center of the whole narrative is money – the money that Pip thinks he is inheriting, which is the same money he forfeits by attempting to save Magwitch's life. The *Bildungsroman*, like most Victorian novels, implicitly or explicitly sets money at the center of the psychological and social drama. It represents a steady paradox inside Victorian fiction and in the minds and hearts of the protagonists. Insofar as money is the direct object of ambition, it is morally destructive. But life inside the new society is brutally inadequate without the money that the protagonists must learn to despise. The upward mobility tale must be modified and compromised – moral education usually comes into sharp conflict with the education required to make a success in the world. And this, in short (and perhaps reductively) is the story of the English *Bildungsroman*.

It is important, before proceeding, however, to note that our contemporary critical argument that these books in English are merely conservative, merely courses in education for the new bourgeoisie, acquiescent in the social norms, even those they seem to criticize, is severely limited. As imaginative explorations of the predicaments and the persistent problems both of the system and of the individual working within the system, these books, at their best, allow for the very insights that they would seem themselves to ignore. That Wemmick is, in his divided self, all of a piece with the system that forces the division is part of the remarkable creative imagination of the book, whatever its "moral" might seem to be. *Great Expectations* does not moralize to us; it invites us, through its language and vision, to imagine ourselves into the condition of confronting the "system," if that's what it should be called, by imagining ourselves into the unique consciousness of a boy learning to maneuver through it. The English *Bildungsroman* speaks in its moment, and at the same time of its moment, and thrusts us into new imaginations of childhood and maturity.

In tracing the movement from childhood to youth to maturity, the *Bildungsroman* gives dramatic shape to the fact that identity, vocation, and social status are no longer merely inherited, but are rather attainments of aspiring individuality in its encounters with new economic and social realities. The Victorian focus on youth and the growth to maturity corresponds, historically, with the growth of the novel form itself, and the shape of that form can be seen to correspond to the radical social transformations which it attempts to absorb and, in England at least, even domesticate. Questions of power and class and even personal identity were at stake in the development of the child to maturity.

The fact that such narratives are representative is attested to by the pervasiveness of the form in Victorian literature. For students of literature and for the general public, thinking about the Victorian novel means necessarily thinking about books like *David Copperfield* and *Jane Eyre*, almost perfect examples of the male and female forms of the subgenre. Of course, there are many others, most of them among the best-known works of the period – George Eliot's *The Mill on the Floss*, for example, or George Meredith's *The Ordeal of Richard Feverel*. Other novels, like Elizabeth Gaskell's beautiful short work, *Cousin Phyllis*, or Thackeray's

Pendennis, which parallels *David Copperfield* in many remarkable ways and was published about the same time, deserve the kind of attention their more famous brothers and sisters have acquired.

And the basic model of the *Bildung* emerges in other novels with ostensibly other things on their minds – think of the story of Dorothea Brooke in *Middlemarch* (which might be taken not as *Bildungsroman* but as a compendium of *Bildungsromane*, as it traces the stories of Lydgate, Fred Vincy, Mary Garth, and Dorothea). Among those non-*Bildung* narrations that are preoccupied with *Bildung* issues, one might number Anthony Trollope's *Phineas Finn* or Gaskell's *North and South* or Meredith's *Beauchamp's Career*. Elizabeth Barrett Browning's almost epic poem, *Aurora Leigh*, is a poet's *Jane Eyre*, and one can find similar patterns, handled of course quite differently, even in "sensation novels," like Willie Collins' *Moonstone* or *Woman in White*, or in that strange half "sensation," half Trollopean novel, *Salem Chapel* (1863), by Margaret Oliphant. And one finds intimations of *Bildung*, in non-realist modes, even in *Wuthering Heights*, where Catherine and Heathcliff do not exactly achieve Victorian "maturity," but where their enigmatic childhoods are the most intensely registered and significant portions of their narrated lives. Although the vogue of the *Bildungsroman* diminished by the end of the century, two classics of their moment stand at the far end of the period as perfectly representative. Mary Augusta (Mrs. Humphrey) Ward's *Robert Elsmere* (1888) was an enormous success as it traced the spiritual (and family) life of a gifted young man who virtually embodies the entire history of religious crisis of the period in moral adventures. It is significant of the centrality of the *Bildungsroman* to Victorian fiction and culture that Ward's great success with the form was precisely representative of a central moral crisis of the period; and the book is further striking in including parallel *Bildung* narratives, particularly of Robert's gifted sister-in-law, Rose. But finally, there is Hardy's last full novel, *Jude the Obscure* (1896), which might be taken as the last of the Victorian *Bildung*, and a kind of reversal of and elegy for the form and its essentially optimistic implications. It is a kind of anti-*Bildung* in which the usual narrative of childish romantic ambition is reversed. That is, as Jude tries to accomplish his childhood ambition of becoming a don at Oxford, as he moves from country to city, he sinks deeper and deeper into misfortune. Class, power, sexuality, all leave Jude defeated, and the happy *Bildung* ending leaves Jude isolated, dying, his life a failure, and his *Bildung* having brought him less than nothing. But, as we have seen in the first chapter, the form in one way or other survived even Hardy, and the self-evidently modernist writer James Joyce exploits the traditions of the form in *Portrait of the Artist as a Young Man* (1916).

II

No two English novels more fully embody the conventions and the implications of the *Bildung* form than *Jane Eyre* and *David Copperfield*. Although there is no need to analyze once again books so frequently interpreted and so deeply engrained in the culture of English speaking people, attention to those aspects of these books that are most characteristic of the conventions of the English *Bildungsroman* will allow further consideration of its social and literary implications and should help emphasize what is so strikingly original and unusual about it. Juxtaposing them, moreover, will help focus differences between male and female *Bildung*. The *Bildungsroman* has traditionally been regarded as a form concerned with the education and formation of men, but in fact in England it is almost equally about women, whose development in the newly emerging bourgeois society was similarly problematic, but in different ways. For every *David Copperfield* there is a *Jane Eyre*, for every *Pendennis* there is a *Mill on the Floss*. While the male *Bildung* concentrates on the upward mobility of the young man making his way in Victorian society, the female version, because women have no such economic mobility, tends to focus on the possibility of a good marriage: women are not so much liberated by the new social and economic systems as reconstrained. They have very little opportunity for development through a vocation, and thus their moral and romantic crises are quite different from those of the men – different but parallel. It would seem that the central drama of the woman's *Bildung* would have to spin around the heroine's getting the "right" man because upward mobility for the woman would depend entirely on her marrying the right man, and to a certain extent that is true.

Nevertheless, the preoccupation with what to do, which we have noted is so central to Victorian narratives, affects both male and female protagonists. Although female *Bildungsromane* ostensibly build their plots around this kind of story, stories that echo with Jane Austen's kind of romance, women too must ask that critical question – both moral and vocational – "What can I do?" "Doing," it turns out, defines them as fully as "doing" defines the men. The question of vocation – what to do for a living – blends with the question of vocation – what to do morally – in many famous narratives. Most famously perhaps in *Jane Eyre*, but even more forcefully in *Villette* (1853), and in George Eliot's *Daniel Deronda*, in which Gwendolen's critical choice is between becoming a governess and marrying corruptly, or, in a now much less well-known book, Dinah Mulock Craik's *Olive* (1850). There the protagonist, Olive, a woman with artistic genius and inherited deformity, has a vocation that works both financially and morally, and that allows her finally to be the devoted artist and the spiritually triumphant lover. Women's choices of worldly success seem to be constricted to marriage, domestic employment, or art (consider also Elizabeth Barrett Browning's *Aurora Leigh*). But on the whole, while for men what they "do" is likely to be work by which they earn a living; for women, it is likely to be moral choosing and resistance.

Both *Jane Eyre* and *David Copperfield* plunge without preliminaries into their narratives – Dickens starting at the very instant of the birth of David, Brontë dropping us *in medias res*, the moment of the developing battle between little Jane and the family of her Aunt Reid, who has taken her in unwillingly. The immediacy of narration is unusual in these works and suggests something of the originality and power of the *Bildungsroman* in its moment. The immediacy derives from the way the narration thrusts the reader inside the worldview of the child – as we have seen already in the discussion of *Great Expectations* – seeing it not as "cute" or charming but as a deeply felt experience, particularly of threats and dangers and unrationalized feeling. Although the narratives are supposed to be written by the mature Jane and David – the Jane who begins the last chapter with "Reader, I married him," and the successful novelist, David Copperfield, who sees his beloved Agnes beside him as he finishes his writing for the evening – both narrators leap imaginatively back into childhood and largely refrain from intruding their mature voices into the dramatization of the experiences of the child. Outside of poetry – for example, Wordsworth's notorious "We Are Seven" – this mode of narration was startlingly original, however commonplace it may seem to modern readers. It controls the point of view so as to render the innocence and limits of the child's vision, while the mature reader, feeling what the child feels, must learn to temper a deeper and broader vision with the frightening reality of the child's perceptions. The effect, of course, is to align the reader with the child through an act of imaginative sympathy. What matters is not the fuller knowledge that comes with maturity, but the child.

Childhood is rendered so intensely and pervasively because it is the condition of promise and potentiality; it enacts the developing social condition of that growing mass of people who have lived past the old feudal order of stable and hereditary social hierarchy. In the *Bildung* form, children are more than children. They are figures who can most fully play out the new instabilities of the social order, the potentialities for movement and growth and upward mobility, and the threatening nature of the world in which these new movements must take place. Their lives imply at least tentative answers to the question of how one might move beyond the limits of the past socially static ways of being. In the context of a newly developing social order in which things are being stood on their head – as the young Pip was forced to perceive them – childhood is the time of a new vision, and is the perfect narrative embodiment of the instability of the old order and the changes that were in the process of overthrowing it. "The more a society perceives itself as a system still unstable and precariously legitimized," says Franco Moretti, "the fuller and stronger the image of youth."[5]

Moretti's argument that the English *Bildungsroman* is a fundamentally conservative genre, working as a kind of handbook for the new bourgeoisie, seems to be confirmed by *David Copperfield* and *Jane Eyre*. Both of these books dramatize and implicitly endorse the compromises necessary to achieve maturity; they wind down their narratives in unqualified acquiescence in those compromises, seeming to affirm the values of the society within which both David and Jane have had to struggle. Their lives have been lessons in how to be bourgeois in these newfangled times, and something they have to learn on their own since they are both, as usual, orphans.

But part of the excitement of the *Bildungsroman* for its contemporary readers is that it did not feel "conservative," but exciting imaginations of new ways of seeing the world, morally forceful exposures of taken-for-granted injustices, and explorations of possibilities. Certainly, the reception of *Jane Eyre* emphasized its rebellious elements and saw Jane as fiery, bold, and even immoral in her determination to assert and maintain her own pride.[6] The retroactive sense we have of their conservatism may be justified by the clear evidence that the books implied the values of the culture that would become dominant, however much the protagonists were dramatized as underdogs; but that sense is not true to the feeling of struggle that belongs to the life of the protagonists, all of whom must, on their own (or virtually) figure out what to do and then go on to do it without being undercut by a world that – however charming it can seem – is full of self-interested and often cruel figures. These novels, if they conclude by reconciling their protagonists with their societies, are thick with evidences of the corruptions and inhumanity of those societies. The condition of the child as helpless emphasizes the arbitrary and often selfish cruelty of the surrounding world and makes of the *Bildung* struggle a constant willed resistance to the social order that, in our current readings, we believe the books are also endorsing. The *Bildung* narrative tends to be a narrative of resistances, not acquiescences, though the novels as a whole virtually define maturity as a willingness to accept the realities and make one's compromises with them. Indeed, they have about them something of the structure and feeling of the fairy-tale, a notoriously violent form even if that form always issues in "poetic justice."

Consider some obvious but now critically understated facts of the almost systematically nasty worlds into which Jane and David are born. In her aunt's home Jane is tyrannized over and ignored or abused daily, and so that opening on the rainy day in which there was no possibility of taking a walk registers the very normality of Jane's existence. It is a normality of the bullying and tyrannizing that first sends her into the Red Room, a kind of dramatic crystallization of the oppression undergone daily. "Forgive me," pleads the innocent Jane to her viciously unjust aunt, "I cannot endure it."[7] But she does and must. The school is no better, of course. At each stage of Jane's troubles the book does allow some softening, but always by figures who are themselves powerless against the dominant structures. First, there is the caring figure of Bessie, and afterwards of Miss Temple and Helen Burns at the school, each in effect teaching lessons of passivity that are inadequate to the violence inflicted. The heroine, to survive, needs not to be Helen Burns, not passive, not unwilling to resist.

Interestingly, David's attractiveness throughout the book is dependent, for the reader, on his initial helplessness and innocence, for the young David Copperfield is put upon and maltreated by everyone but his mother and Peggoty through the entire first part of the book. As a young man and adult, David remains largely passive, even in his strenuous escape to find Aunt Betsy. The world around him is governed by self-interest and regardlessness of others' pain, and success in it is obviously determined by one's skill in outwitting others, particularly the innocent. But David is never allowed to compete in that world, not even in his maturity, and when he follows out the desires of his "undisciplined heart," he marries absolutely the wrong woman, almost destroys his life, and must be rescued by Dickens' plotting to kill Dora early.

A fundamental structural difference between the two books might be directly traced to the gender difference. *Jane Eyre* is always about Jane Eyre. On the contrary, although David's "undisciplined heart" and the narrative of his relations with various women, Little Emily, Rosa Dartle, Dora Spenlow, and Agnes, runs throughout the book, there are a series of sub-narratives that take over – Steerforth's elopement with Emily (with an implicit but not developed implication of David's guilt for introducing Steerforth to the Peggotys); the Peggotys' pursuit of Emily and the ultimate dramatic and powerfully rendered death of Steerforth; the moral collapse of Mr. Wickfield before Uriah Heep's intricate plotting; Heep's conspiracy and ultimate exposure by Micawber; the implicit adultery narrative of Annie Strong. Each one of these narratives plays out what might legitimately be taken as an aspect of David's desires and failings – Steerforth runs off with the little girl David had played with and loved; Heep lusts after Agnes, the woman every reader knows soon enough will be the woman David marries and whom David really loves; Annie Strong seems implicated (incorrectly it turns out) in an adulterous relation with Muldoon. There is no need to elaborate on the possible implications of all these narratives: the point is that for much of the book, despite occasional outbursts of rage against Heep (whose false humility is the other side of the supposed real humility that the book's ideal posits), the focus shifts from David; his problems are displaced onto others so that in the narrative itself he does not really have to take initiative and engage with the nasty world the book has revealed from the earliest chapters. For the most part David remains a much more passive figure than Jane, whose passivity is all derived from external constraints or from her willed internalization of the world's moral values, but who is never morally passive.

That the sins and the redemptions *David Copperfield* narrates are all played out by others is symptomatic of that widely recognized characteristic of Victorian fiction and particularly of this subgenre, the incapacity of novelists to imagine a forceful, active male character who is not either corrupting (like Steerforth) or corrupted. Dickens' career as a novelist can almost be measured by the way his male protagonists, in *Bildung*-like narratives, avoid corruption. In *Oliver Twist*, Oliver is absolutely unstained by experience and remains the passive innocent who is not responsible for any of his problems and lives happily ever after; in *David Copperfield*, David's potential guilts are played out in the actions of other characters, as I have already suggested, but those guilts do indeed hover about the narrative. He is, moreover, guilty of an "undisciplined heart." (That phrase, which David uses about himself, neatly diagnoses the problems of many *Bildung* heroes and of the protagonists of realist fiction since *Don Quixote*.) Only in *Great Expectations*, written almost a decade after *David Copperfield*, does Dickens create a *Bildung* protagonist who is genuinely "guilty," who loses his innocence and can be redeemed only by acting at the sacrifice of his wealth. To enter the new world is to open oneself to corruption; to act in it is almost inevitably to be corrupted. Only by creating a passive figure whom fate treats kindly, or by displacing moral failings onto others in the story, can Dickens (or almost any Victorian novelist) create a male protagonist who is both thoroughly decent and materially successful.

The gender difference lies in the fact that Jane has no choice but to be passive, and yet her narrative is alive and original just because, within the constraints and ideals imagined for Victorian women, she is insistently herself and refuses to defer to anyone beyond the required limits. She keeps making demands for herself. Rochester falls in love with her because he detects that strength and knows that she will not falsely acquiesce in convention or defer to him where she thinks him wrong or misguided. St John Rivers is astonished at her directness: "He had not imagined that a woman would dare to speak so to a man." And Rivers tells her that "You are original . . . and not timid. There is something brave in your spirit, as well as penetrating in your eye" (ch. 32). Jane's great attractiveness and power reside in the fact that she is never morally or psychologically passive, no matter how circumstances confine her; but David is a man and his passivity is thus the condition of his virtue in the novelist's imagined world. David as an abused and helpless child can be passive because he is a child, but passivity is the mark of his maturity as well. He does not, after his escape from the blacking factory and the great good fortune of his finding his Aunt Betsy, make anything happen. He is an observer. Jane, on the other hand, has to resist at every moment and must, at the critical moment, make her choices and do something.

At the crisis of *Jane Eyre*, as happens with many heroines of many Victorian novels, Jane, having learned that Rochester is married, asks that critical Victorian question, "What am I to do?" (ch. 27, p. 335). Against the seductive appeals of Rochester she acts, almost to the point of death, and wanders off penniless and without direction until she is saved by her cousins. This unlikely rescue at the edge of death and despair has often been taken as a fairy-tale intervention of Brontë's, and certainly, the book has described a world in which only by some great good fortune beyond the reach of good character can good character be saved. In that sense, the world is rather like the world of *David Copperfield*. It is of some real importance to our understanding of the Victorian novel that the question of what to do is posed exactly between the desire to satisfy worldly passions and the desire to hold true to a religious faith that often implies an impractical moral vigor. The religious choice is supported here (and essential to the conception of Jane's character) only by plotting that has to imply divine providence. The realist novel tries for the most part to do without such plotting, or, perhaps more precisely, tries to plot its narratives in such a way that the secular likelihood converges with the religious resolution. But there is a tension in Victorian realist fiction between the kind of art that would support the realist vision and the kind of art that implies a transcendent power in a world that contradicts the assumptions of a strict realism. Supernatural intervention feels, in the context of realist fiction, to be something out of a different genre, the fairy-tale perhaps. The reconciliation between the ideal of a morally ordered world and a secularly chancy one is almost always strained. The tension is embodied in Jane's choice: the choice to leave Rochester and her worldly desire and love requires a plot device that in ordinary secular terms would seem the introduction of a radical and thoroughly unlikely coincidence.

David's flight is, in a way, the reverse of Jane's. His is self-protective, and he knows where he is going, difficult as the trip may be. His trip across Southern England to his aunt's house is a remarkable piece of writing marked by a series of funny and painful episodes that are thoroughly consistent with the vision of a predatory world, already adumbrated in the book. For the most part it is seen through the eyes of the innocent young David, who is consistently duped and exploited and can, in the face of such heartlessness, retain his innocence. Nevertheless, while there is no radical coincidence that pulls David through, the narrative allows the happy conclusion and, in another way, a secular way, rewards the protagonist.

Once "saved," David falls in love (several times), unable to control and discipline his heart, but he has no control over the events that become the focus of the book. He cannot keep Heep from exploiting Mr. Wickfield and threatening to win Agnes. He works hard, but largely offstage. He is incapable of managing his household (all the blame laid on Dora's silliness and innocence). The novel's subject interest seems to switch from David to the other major figures so that the first sentence of the novel raises what turns out to become a real question – "WHETHER I shall turn out to be the hero of my own life, or whether that station will be held by anybody else, these pages must show." Whereas, in the long run, the *Bildungsroman* spins around the question of work, "What shall I do?" is both a literal question about work and a moral question. The way characters answer that question determines their capacity to survive in the modern world but also raises the issues of the relation between material and moral success. Male protagonists have far more opportunity to drift and slip into that sort of maturity that allows them to cope satisfactorily with contemporary reality. Female protagonists, constrained like Jane to choices between being a governess and marrying, at every point must make firm choices and can't afford the sorts of mistakes that David makes right from the start. Jane must have the strength to resist, first, Rochester, when she discovers he is married, and then St John Rivers, whom she doesn't love but whose self-sacrificing work she was willing to assume. Each negation is a positive act marking Jane as that strong morally independent figure that has turned the novel into a key text for modern feminism.

But David's passivity is not explicitly recognized by the narrative and is the quality that allows Dickens to sustain the sense of his moral innocence in the midst of so fraught and potentially corrupt a world, with its Murdstones and Heeps and Muldoons and Spenlows and even Steerforths. It is centrally significant that despite what he knows of Steerforth, David deeply loves him. The book both disguises and makes plain that the energies and desires that drive Steerforth are potential in David. The displacement of the story in the second half of the book to these other characters – to Steerforth, and Micawber and Heep and Mr. Wickfield – diverts the development of the novel in such a way that David never has to confront his own capacity for the kinds of things that Steerforth (who runs off with the girl David first loves) and Heep (who lusts after the women he ends loving) do.

This outline is too simple to do justice to the nuances of the narratives, but it is striking how parallel the lines of the story of Jane and David run. And it is yet more striking how intensely the narratives focus on the consciousnesses and the perceptions of the two protagonists. Even as things slip from bad to worse, the very nature of the narrative celebrates the selfhood of these two figures. Brontë lets Jane look with a deeply subjective vision, but achieves a remarkable objectivity of representation in so doing. So Jane notes how, locked in the Red Room, she spied her face in the mirror and saw a "strange little figure there gazing at me, with a white face and arms specking the gloom, and glittering eyes of fear moving where all else was still" (ch. 2, p. 21). Such a passage both insists on the emotional experience of the child and registers a reality that the adult reader can translate sympathetically. The *Bildungsroman* depends on the assumption that the personal, distinctively individual, sharply defined selfhood is the true subject, and that the narrative excitement derives from that self's power to contest and ultimately come to terms with the social and political conditions that constantly threaten it.

It is important to note, however, the way the parallels, marking certain general qualities of the Victorian *Bildungsroman*, are not quite parallel. It is true that both children are orphans, both oppressed at home and then in rigidly brutal schools, where education is merely submission and itself entirely corrupt, both thrown into demeaning worlds of work, both, at different stages of their lives, forced to wander desperately through a hostile landscape that threatens quite literally to kill them, both saved almost miraculously by relatives who take them in. And both, in the end, are saved, David from his mistakes, Jane from the pure self-assertive integrity of her refusals: David marries Agnes and settles into the bourgeois order and domestic comfort that, a modern reader must recognize, is largely a protected denial of the crass realities of the Heeplike world, that is everywhere beyond the ordered domestic world; Jane can fulfill her secular passion for a worldly lover in terms that are fully reconciled with the religious faith that, at one point, turned her away from him. They learn to make their compromises with a threateningly hostile world and to affirm, in the end, the selves that have carried them through all difficulties.

By the time of Hardy's *Jude the Obscure*, the *Bildungsroman*, as a mode that maneuvers successfully around the brutalities of the world it is designed to humanize, has become virtually impossible. The tensions implicit in the form are, in *Jude the Obscure*, made to dominate and ultimately ruin the protagonists' lives. Jude finds no Aunt Betsy to support him – Jude's aunt, though sympathetic, is merely a choral warning; Sue Bridehead's daring – Jane-Eyrelike – intellect does nothing to protect her either from her own complex and contradictory feelings or from the society in which she finally acquiesces. But acquiescence here is no product of maturity and the realist will to compromise. It is a total and debasing surrender, made appalling to reader and protagonist. And Jude's great expectations leave him dying alone beyond the ken or concern of the celebrating Christminster crowds. Hardy makes something powerful out of the *Bildung* materials once again, but only by resisting the conventions that gave to Jane and David their happy and compromised endings. By the end of the nineteenth century, the freedom implicit in the conception of child protagonists had largely lost its energy; another freer floating and yet no less oppressive economic and social order had locked firmly in place; the romantic aspirations that would lead *Bildung* protagonists to some kind of moral and material success in the newly forming bourgeois culture had lost their charm, and Hardy's "Old Father Time," Jude's son without Jude's romantic dreams, sees that we are, in this world, "too many." Jane and David are no longer imaginable, except with a touch of nostalgia. The Victorian *Bildung* had in effect run its course, though its powerful emphasis on the nature and integrity of individual identity, its focus on the imagination of the growing child and on the dream of possibilities, remains a great gift to the tradition of the English novel.

Notes

1 In the eighteenth century the concern with youth and even with childhood was already blossoming, but if we take that marvelous aberration, *Tristram Shandy* (1767), as an example, we can find that narratives starting from the very beginning, from birth, are doing very different sorts of work from that done by the nineteenth-century versions. Tristram's life is traced even back to conception, and its wild comic eccentricity is far less concerned with the child's vision than with the satiric comic vision of the author. In fact, Tristram himself is not born until well into the novel and he is not the focus of attention except as the book gives us a good deal about his "opinions," and much more about Uncle Toby and Walter Shandy than about himself.

2 There has been a large developing literature on the female *Bildung*. For an early summary and bibliography, see Laura Sue Federer, *The Female Bildungsroman in English: An Annotated Bibliography of Criticism* (New York: Publications of the Modern Language Association, 1990).

3 Franco Moretti, *The Way of the World: The Bildungsroman in European Culture* (London: Verso, 1987), p. 3.

4 See Moretti, *The Way of the World*; D. A. Miller, *The Novel and the Police* (Berkeley: University of California Press, 1988); Jerome Hamilton Buckley, *Season of Youth: The Bildungsroman from Dickens to Golding* (Cambridge, MA: Harvard University Press, 1974). Buckley offers an older view that does not emphasize the conservatism. But note this by Lennard Davis, *Resisting Novels* (New York: Methuen, 1987): "The form, by and large, is one that fundamentally resists change. To argue that the novel can defy its defensive function is to argue that horses are born

without legs – it happens, but not often, and then in spite of formal requirements"
(p. 22).

5   Moretti, *The Way of the World*, p. 185.

6   Some contemporaries were shocked by Jane's boldness and self-assertiveness, by,
that is, the very qualities (combined, of course, with a great deal of obedient
respect) that attract Rochester to her. The fact that Jane is a woman obviously
accounts for this sense of excessive pride and rebelliousness. That the young David
Copperfield tried to resist the oppression of the Murdstones and of his work in the
city arouses no such objections among critics, but seems utterly right to everyone.

7   *Jane Eyre* (London: Penguin Books, 2003), p. 24.

Chapter 5

The Sensation Novel and
The Woman in White

I

If the tendency has long been to think of the Victorians as prudish and constrained, unwilling to confront sexuality and almost obsessively pre-occupied with truthfulness, the flourishing of the "sensation novel"[1] in the 1860s suggests that the tendency is at least partly misguided. Sensation fiction did evoke cries of alarm, in particular from highbrow critics, but it was enormously popular, and it built its plots around murder, fraud, false identities, profligate sexuality, divorce, bigamy, cold-blooded poisoning, elaborate conspiracies. Of course, there was no pornography, not even soft pornography, but it's clear enough that some of the figures in these novels were up to no sexual good.

It all began – the story goes – in 1860, in Dickens' new journal, *All the Year Round*, when Wilkie Collins' *The Woman in White* began weekly serialization and ran from November 26, 1859 through August 25, 1860. The book was a smash. But Collins' novel only brought to a focus concerns that were never far from the surface of the most classic of Victorian novels. In *All the Year Round*, which replaced his earlier journal, *Household Words*, Dickens emphasized the publication of serial novels, a move that turned out to be highly successful and lucrative, no issue ever selling fewer than 100,000 copies. It guaranteed a wide readership to Collins' novel, which was one of the first to appear, and that in turn bolstered the journal in its early days. *The Woman in White* was a cliff-hanger, and it was full of complex plotting, characters with assumed identities, false imprisonment, bigamy, death by fire, and international intrigue. This is not exactly conservative and prudish Victorian fare, but it found a very large and enthusiastic audience that waited anxiously from week to week for further developments.

In the preface to the one-volume edition of the book, published when the serial was completed, Collins was confident enough about its success in serial form that he could write that "this volume scarcely stands in need of any prefatory introduction." He did not restrain himself, however, from providing a brief rationale for his literary method: "I have always held the old-fashioned opinion that the primary object of a work of fiction should be to tell a story."[2] While this sounds innocent enough, it points to what was thought to be the fundamental difference between the "sensation novel," as it was recognized by the critics, and the realist novel, which by the 1860s had thoroughly dominated the English literary market. The comment goes to justify the serial mode of publishing – which was, for the most part, taken by serious critics as inferior art. But as we have seen, a significant portion of classic Victorian novels had also been published serially – even George Eliot's *Romola*, *Middlemarch*, and *Daniel Deronda*.

Nevertheless, Collins' explicit commitment to the priority of "story" does put him slightly at odds with his realist contemporaries. Telling a story was not the primary objective of mainstream realism, which required, first of all, strong development of "character." The ideal, however, was to make the story grow with a sense of inevitability out of the interaction of the characters, which was forcefully articulated later in the century by Henry James,[3] in whose prefaces to his novels written long after their initial publication he described processes that invariably worked from an almost instantaneous intuition of character in a charged moment to elaborate plots that the character's nature itself would seem to have generated. Character was the focus – for Thackeray, for George Eliot, for Anthony Trollope, and even, despite the narrative fireworks and the comparative "flatness" of his protagonists, for Dickens. Ironically, Collins himself insisted on the primacy of character, noting that "it is not possible to tell a story successfully without presenting characters . . . The only narrative that can hope to lay a strong hold on the attention of readers is a narrative which interests them about men and women" (p. 12).

Despite the contemporary furor, the sensation novel was not so much an aberration from as it was a particular inflection of the dominant realist mode, which had always included its share of the scandalous. But the sensation novel foregrounded material that in domestic realism tended to be repressed or to be recognized immediately as beyond the pale or disguised. In his autobiography, Anthony Trollope, the realist *par excellence* and the novelist least interested in worrying the reader about the "story," addressed the point directly.

> Among English novels of the day, and among English novelists, a great division is made. There are sensational novels and anti-sensational; sensational readers and anti-sensational. The novelists who are considered to be anti-sensational are generally called realistic. I am realistic. My friend Wilkie Collins is generally supposed to be sensational. The readers who prefer the one are supposed to take delight in the elucidation of character. They who hold by the other are charmed by the construction and gradual development of plot.[4]

This distinction, however, Trollope recognizes as inadequate, for he continues:

> All this is, I think, a mistake, – which mistake arises from the inability of the imperfect artist to be at the same time realistic and sensational. A good novel should be both, and both in the highest degree. If a novel fail in either there is a failure in art.

Trollope proceeds to hammer home his point by alluding to a series of scenes in Scott, in *Jane Eyre*, and in Thackeray's *Henry Esmond*.

But one need not stop with them. I have argued at length elsewhere that underneath the surface of every realist novel there is a "monster" waiting to get out.[5] Under the valued domesticity there are desires and energies restrained by the conventions of Victorian realism and by the developing conventions of Victorian society. Look closely, as realists required themselves to do, at any quiet domestic situation and there would suddenly appear secret pasts and non-domestic lives, "other Victorians," untold narratives. The sensation/realism distinction doesn't hold because the central qualities of the sensation novel – its emphasis on intrigue, its focus on behavior beyond the bounds of ostensibly decent social order, its revelation of dirty secrets, its suspenseful registration of mysteries – are virtually always also aspects of the realist novel. It is true that the sensation novel lingers over the wicked and the dangerous, and makes it the primary focus of its narrative, but it is a difference in emphasis not in content. The sensation novel takes the conditions of ordinary bourgeois life on which the realistic novel focuses and shows them to be mere surfaces above a world of energies and desires that are distinctly not domestic. The sensation novel was so disturbing to so many people (and so attractive to so many others) just because it exploited the conventions of realism and set the mysteries and desires and disruptions inside the domestic.

Very shortly after *The Woman in White* appeared in *All the Year Round*, Dickens began publishing what might well be his most "realistic" book, or at least the one that most consistently imagines and develops character – *Great Expectations* (1861). While we have seen it as a quintessential *Bildungsroman* and noted how steeped it is in realistic representation of character, it was taken by many as another sensation novel. And that is not entirely unfair. It too was published in weekly installments, it too features an attack and murder; it brings convicts into the drawing room, and in Miss Havisham, as many critics have noted, there is probably an echo of the woman in white of Collins' novel. What could be more grotesque than the life of the decaying jilted lady; and what could more forcefully bring home the degree of crime and dishonor that underlay civil society than Mr. Jaggers' frightening (and secretive) knowledge? Despite the dramatic opening with the escaped convict, despite the grotesquerie of the Miss Havisham plot, even despite the attack on Pip's sister, in retrospect the book seems no more exaggerated (rather less so), no more preoccupied with "sensational" subjects, than any other of Dickens' great works. In dramatizing for the young Pip the way in which the world of violence and criminality underlies the most attractive and interesting of romances, *Great Expectations* plays out one of the dominant themes of both realist and sensation fiction. And perhaps the first serious literary detective, Mr. Bucket, turns up in *Bleak House* (1853), which features also the anonymous death of Nemo, the murder of Tulkinghorn, a bastard heroine and an adulterous mother, among other things. Brutal sadists abound – in *Nicholas Nickleby* (1839), for instance. *Oliver Twist* is also a bastard, and he spends much of his time with a gang of pickpockets, while the violent beating of Nancy by Sikes – written in the 1830s not in the 1860's, the time of the flourishing of the sensation novel – became a set piece of Dickens' readings, and caused the fainting of many women in his audiences. The catalogue could go on, and might conclude with the various murders and assaults that mark *Our Mutual Friend* (1865), but would include an adultery plot (to be sure, not fulfilled) in *Dombey and Son* (1848) and in *Hard Times* (1854), Little Emily's sexual liaison with Steerforth in *David Copperfield* (1850), and the drug smoking in *Edwin Drood* (1870). Dickens may not qualify as a realist in the same way

George Eliot does, but he claimed, even for the scene of spontaneous human combustion in *Bleak House*, that he was being true to life.

Consider some of the other great classics of Victorian literature that have helped establish its reputation for sexual and moral restraint. We have seen that Thackeray's *Vanity Fair* gives us a heroine with a vaguely falsified name, who, the reader is led to believe, has committed adultery with Lord Steyne and flirts adulterously with George Osborne, who kills Amelia's brother Jos, and who, for her troubles, lives happily ever after doing charity work. One might argue that Becky and *Vanity Fair* are exceptional, and that in the end, the narrator comes down strongly for the virtue (that he does not show triumphant). But Thackeray was not by any means alone.

For a full understanding of the way Victorian fiction works, it is necessary to attend to what is repressed or understated or treated as aberration. The quiet, sexually tranquil, and entirely domestic world of Victorian realism depends on instabilities and excesses that it will, in whatever hedged terms, formally renounce. This is true even for Trollope's deliberately unagitated and stylistically simple narratives, so explicitly realistic and anti-sensational. While he absolutely and repeatedly rejected the idea that he should ever keep his readers hanging, as Dickens and Collins most deliberately did, much of the fascination of his work depends nevertheless on threats of violence and disruption, even sexual threats. In the novel that made his reputation, *Barchester Towers*, there is the brilliantly conceived figure of Madame Neroni, who has been crippled by a brutal assault by her Italian husband, and who returns to Barchester to seduce any man who comes within reach. Most of the sequences that feature her are played in a comic mode as she toys with her own sexuality and her respectable suitors' evident illegitimate desire. The fact of sexuality is inescapable, and yet Madame Neroni emerges far more sympathetically than, in a non-sensational Victorian novel, any such exploiter of sexuality ostensibly should. *The Eustace Diamonds* (1873) could easily pass for a sensation novel. The great sequence of the Palliser novels virtually begins, in *Can You Forgive Her?* (1864), with the very near miss of adulterous relations between Palliser's wife, Cora, and young handsome Burgo, whom she loves. The subplot of the novel includes a dangerous and potentially violent quasi-villain, George Vavasor. The other novels include suicides and murders and madness. Realism couldn't get on without such things, nor could the Victorian novel.

Elizabeth Gaskell's novels would seem at least safe from the inroads of sensation and violence and scandal, but of course this is not the case. Her two important industrial novels, *Mary Barton* (1848) and *North and South* (1855), include murder – and, indeed, Mary Barton's story is built around murder – and mutiny and not quite accidental death and worker riots. It is certainly true that Gaskell focuses on the domestic, and attempts to tame or punish excess, most strikingly, even excessively, in *Ruth* (1853). But the story of Ruth is the story of an illegitimate sexual relationship, and an illegitimate child, and while Gaskell relentlessly pursues Ruth, most particularly for allowing herself to lie about her past, the book once again depends on material that would become grist for sensation fiction.

Yet even the great Victorian theorist and exemplar of moral realism, George Eliot, who criticized silly women novelists for filling their books with romance and the extraordinary, filled her novels with sensational material. We have illicit sex and baby murder in *Adam Bede* (1859), violent death and quasi-adulterous behavior in *Mill on the Floss* (1860), drug addiction and robbery in *Silas Marner* (1861), adultery, illegitimacy, and violent and deadly riot in *Felix Holt* (1866), patricide and adultery in *Romola* (1863), swindling, theft of inheritance, and death from alcoholism in *Middlemarch* (1872), and identity problems, gambling, theft, and the death of an adulterous villain at sea in *Daniel Deronda* (1876). More interestingly yet, the introduction of these elements into the novels sometimes was in the service of plot manipulation one would have thought inconsistent with the realist ideal – the great flood that kills Maggie Tulliver is the most obvious such plotting device. There is an important sequence in *Middlemarch* in which the narrator needs to justify the "chance" events that lead to the exposure of the hypocritical banker Bulstrode, but we will reserve discussion of this until the next chapter. And most strikingly of all, there is the revelation of Daniel Deronda's Jewishness – not only the narrative unlikeliness of it, but the strategies of plotting that lead to the revelation. Thus, right in the heart of the most important realistic work of the century, these sensational elements, both of matter and narrative strategy, are evident. And, as Margaret Oliphant points out, sensation novels usually carry within them the kinds of details of bourgeois and respectable life that mark realism. One may be realist, one may be sensational, but there is a remarkable similarity between their worlds; and that in particular is what makes the sensation novel so interesting and apparently disruptive.

In a long essay on the sensation novel, in which she is strongly hostile to the genre, Margaret Oliphant makes an exception of Collins and indicates what it is that makes *The Woman in White* so forceful despite the sordidness of most sensational materials:

> A writer who boldly takes in hand the common mechanism of daily life, and by means of persons who might all be living in society for anything we can tell to the contrary, thrills us into wonder, terror, and breathless interest . . . has accomplished a far greater success than he who effects the same result through supernatural agencies, or by means of the fantastic creations of lawless genius or violent horrors of crime.[6]

It is just because Collins scrupulously adheres to the implicit rules of realist representation that his novel appealed so powerfully to (and repelled) large segments of the Victorian reading population. His novels are filled with details about the objects of domestic life, and in fact, the kind of detective work that some of his characters must do requires intense, let us call it realist, attention to details – the detailism of realism. Collins' narratives thus injected excitement and mystery into the quotidian. Oliphant notes how Collins carefully eschews exaggerations of excitement. Even more strikingly and to the point here, she claims that "there is almost as little that is objectionable in this highly-wrought sensation novel, as if it had been a domestic history of the most gentle and unexciting kind" (p. 113). The strategy that Oliphant rightly describes is one in which the ordinary is mystified, made strange. And although the methods are different and less dramatically striking, this is precisely the major aim of Victorian realism – the ordinary world is made to carry great emotive weight and grand significance. As Henry James put it, "To Mr. Collins belongs the credit of having introduced into fiction those most mysterious of mysteries, the mysteries which are at our own doors."[7]

Both realist novel and sensation novel are committed to an ultimately romantic view that the ordinary is always potentially extraordinary. One can see the world in a grain of sand. One can recognize epic and tragic elements in the workings of everyday life. For the realist, there is a moral mission in demonstrating that the ordinary is as significant as the epic or tragic. The passions that move the carpenter Adam Bede are as important as the passions that moved Oedipus or Hamlet. For the sensation novelist, the everyday, the ordinary, is also loaded with significance, but the objective is not George Eliot's, to make us feel the value and importance of ordinary people. Rather, it seems committed to showing that the ordinary disguises the extraordinary in ways that George Eliot and the other realists did not want to emphasize. The ordinary is not only mined with extravagant feelings and desires (a subject of realist fiction from *Don Quixote* to *Madame Bovary* to *Middlemarch*), but it is dangerous and often nasty.

Where the realist novel romanticizes and emphasizes domesticity with the aim of dramatizing the great value of the domestic, the sensation novel romanticizes it by suggesting that domestic tranquility is either a sham or a very fragile defense against the reality of evil – there is a killer or a lunatic in the drawing room or the kitchen, the very people we spend our lives with may not be who they seem, there might be afoot extraordinary schemes to defraud us, thefts are possible – everything that a strong bourgeois culture would like to believe happens outside domesticity, outside the family, is actually inside it.

If D. A. Miller is right that the Victorian novel is a kind of handbook for middle-class readers, what kind of handbook are these sensation novels? Is the bourgeois life quite as pleasant and comfortable and safe and caring as it looks when we watch the women around the hearth knitting and embroidering and the men reading attentively in their libraries? Of course, in the end, the sensation novel restores order and domestic tranquility, provides the right marriages, punishes the wicked among us, but in the course of its narratives it has done rather too much to suggest that these reinstituted tranquilities are not what they seem. One might say, with the sensation novel, the cat is out of the bag. Why is it, when we are done with them, that the "bad" figures turn out to be the most interesting and that the restored bourgeois world doesn't manage to resolve the deeper issues that propelled the dramatic plots in the first place?

The disruptions that the sensation novel unleashes (and then purports to tame) reflect once again that new destabilization of social order, the new contest for power between the rising middle class and the old aristocracy, the new porousness of class distinctions, and along with these the uncertainty of personal identity in a culture where all individuals have to create themselves, and in which money, as the source of power, figures so prominently. As Ronald Thomas points out, the sensation novel is "always concerned with money and success, elaborate financial intrigues that surround . . . the bourgeois family."[8] The formal features of the sensation novel, insofar as they can be singled out, tend to reflect these thematic (and social) problems; it is a form that unlike the realist novel tends to set its stories in the present, to deal with present issues with the most modern awareness of new developments in science, commerce, and law. It worries technical problems like point of view, which in effect asks how we know what we know; it worries commercial problems, by which money replaces both inheritance and psychological integrity as the determiner of identity, and by which even humans become at times rather little more than currency. The sensation novel was, in a way, the delightful and thrilling nightmare of the new bourgeois order to which the realist novel addressed its primary attention – thrilling because of the pleasures that almost always go with transgression (the most interesting figures in literary history tend to be villains, like Iago, or Satan) and delightful because it seemed to offer a way to resolve the problems that transgression inevitably creates, to re-establish order and establish authenticity.

II

Oliphant's argument about the special originality and strength of *The Woman in White* applies to the sensation novel as a whole, although, while admiring Collins, she despised other representatives of that species.[9] It is true that few sensation novels are as carefully contrived, restrained, and orderly as Collins' two major works in the genre, *The Woman in White* (1860) and *The Moonstone* (1868), but most of them work in roughly similar fashion to trouble the calm surfaces of bourgeois life by revealing the horrors beneath, and that rather helps explain why the form evoked such great hostility (and such popular enthusiasm). Offering Victorian readers a wholly recognizable and ostensibly comfortable world, the sensation novels made all things uncomfortable and in so doing implicitly challenged the dominant assumptions and attitudes of Victorian society. It is just because the sensation novel is much more like the novels of Dickens and George Eliot and Thackeray than contemporary reviewers allowed that it aroused such violently antagonistic feelings.

It is worth lingering over the similarities. Sensation novels are usually not set in exotic places or distant times: they are of the moment, this England, these country estates, these towns, although the exotic on occasion erupts into the familiar landscape, almost becoming a figure for what lies beneath the surface of the respectable world. *The Moonstone* is, perhaps, more explicit than most on the point: "here was our quiet English house suddenly invaded by a devilish Indian Diamond."[10] But then the battle of Waterloo is central to the whole narrative of *Vanity Fair*, the West Indies are crucial to *Jane Eyre*, Mrs. Transome's son's return from India sets going the narration of George Eliot's *Felix Holt* (1866), and his radical politics lead to the unearthing of the fact of his illegitimacy. The political, the alien, and the personal are all entwined in a way that the sensation novel would exploit and develop (and in fact, *Felix Holt* was written in the heart of the sensation decade, the 1860s). The exotic enters in many forms into mainstream realist fiction. In Trollope's *Can You Forgive Her?* (1864) the wild waters of the Swiss mountains open out threateningly the possibility of dangerous personal relationships and dangerously extreme action. Hardy's novels, so tightly set in the English West Country, are full not only of rude and imposing landscapes, of impenetrable woods, and natural dangers, but these almost invariably translate into dangerous and threatening personal relationships and the unearthing of secrets that prove perilous for the protagonists. For the most part, however, as with most of mainstream Victorian fiction, the empire itself usually remains only on the edges of the story.[11] The great difference is that for the sensation novel, focusing on the excitement of the story rather than on the development of "character," the alien and the strange, the scandal and the hidden mystery become far more important than the everyday life they subvert. Although the sensation novels, like their more respectable counterparts, do all resolve by restoring order, each one dramatically represents ways in which the apparent order is latent with disruption and vulnerable to forces, natural and social, that produce scandal, corruption, deceit, and violence. But, for both kinds of novels, the ordinary becomes worryingly alive with dangerous potentialities and becomes extraordinary; the monstrous inhabits both worlds.

It would be wrong, however, to minimize how intensely contemporaries responded to the sensation novel, and saw in it differences that, from a longer perspective, can be seen as similarities. The sensation novel was different, but its similarities to mainstream realism go well beyond realism's interest in the monstrous that lies beneath the surface of the real. Both forms of the novel were clearly responding to the same cultural forces, though in different ways. And that fact is nowhere more evident than in the way sensation novels partake of many of the qualities of the *Bildungsroman*. It doesn't take much to notice that almost all sensation novels have within them a very important *Bildung* narrative. The male protagonists may not be as thoroughly orphaned as are David Copperfield and Jane Eyre, and the reader doesn't meet them until they are past childhood, but they are young men who have not found themselves and who, through the course of the narrative, develop clarity of objective and powers of working efficiently and maturely. Each sensation novel tends to resolve its more or less complex plot through the labors of a young man who matures and becomes worthy of the heroine just in the act of resolving the mystery, or solving the crime. Ronald Thomas has emphasized how insistently concerned with the authority of the new professionals the sensation novel is. The growth to maturity in the new society is a growth to professional mastery, to a way of deciphering the deceits and dangers that underlie the ostensibly respectable surfaces. The *Bildung* hero achieves maturity by becoming a kind of detective. His pursuit of information forces him to develop the investigative skills of a professional, a detective, or lawyer, or even doctor, and his acquired knowledge has professional authority just as the modern world shows itself to be dangerously close to indecipherable.

At the start, Franklin Blake of *The Moonstone* and Robert Audley of *Lady Audley's Secret* are both rather aimless fringe aristocrats. Although the focus of the novels is on uncovering the mystery, who stole the diamond or what happened to Audley's best friend, the narrative is only possible if the young men can be redeemed by their work in a quite Victorian way. They find the answer to the big Victorian question, "What to do?" just by doing, that is, by working very hard at resolving the mysteries. In the act, they mature and they become in a real sense "professional." It is the same old Victorian question, though, that drives their narratives: "What can I do?" or perhaps "Why do anything?" What can provoke them to meaningful work? The mystery and potential scandal in these novels are precisely what prod the men into "doing."

In *The Woman in White*, for example, the plot depends on the character of Hartwright, the lover of Laura Fairlie, later Lady Glyde. Hartwright is an artist, somewhat unusual in these novels because his professional work is what he wants to do. But he is dependent on commissions and his work is sporadic. Although he is offstage in exotic America during the most intense of Count Fosco's manipulations, it is the danger to Laura when he returns (and his desire for her, of course) that drives him into detective action immediately. One might regard *The Woman in White* as his story. In need of money and work, rather innocent in the ways of the world, in the course of the novel he turns not only into the defender of Laura Fairlie, but into a rigorous and relentless investigator who ultimately matures sufficiently to counter the activities of Count Fosco himself and of course to win the heroine. The book itself, a compilation of eyewitness testimonies that he has put together, is the substantive evidence of his development and power. He himself is the first eyewitness. His point of view as a young man opens the story and renders it with something of the immediacy with which *David Copperfield* and *Jane Eyre* open.

As the organizer of the whole story, Hartwright tellingly requires of all the witnesses that he enlists that they write down only what they have experienced directly. The demand is consistent with the empiricism that lies at the philosophical foundation of British realism, but in the very making of the demand Hartwright seems to suggest that any individual point of view would provide only a very limited sense of the events. Although Hartwright eventually succeeds in squeezing a totally coherent story out of his witnesses, the very effort to tell the story in this way calls into question the reliability of empirical knowledge. While the book as a whole – as D. A. Miller argues about *The Moonstone*, which uses a similar narrative strategy – in fact denies the apparent relativity of knowledge by making a single inescapable narrative out of the pieces, the experience of reading at least intimates how very slippery empiricism and experience are as criteria for knowledge. It is necessary to have Hartwright organize the entire narrative, collect each witness's part, and conclude the story himself.

While the ostensible focus of the story is not Hartwright's education and maturity, the novel narrates his growth, and by making him confront a lover and a villainous plot against her, gives him a reason to engage with the world more seriously than his work as artist seems to require. The advance to maturity is marked by his power to elicit the various narrative pieces and then by his power to use what they reveal to make a shapely whole of a story that threatens to escape control. His work is to establish the identity of his wife, very distinctly the work of a lawyer, though he remains an artist too.

It is the same story, with a slightly different twist, in *Lady Audley's Secret.* In that novel Robert Audley, who "was supposed to be a barrister,"[12] must turn himself into a detective, maturing from the insouciant careless-ness and lack of commitment of his youth as a charming aimless bachelor to a shrewd if passionate detective ready to expose Lady Audley and, in the end, responsible for putting her away in a madhouse. Robert is already a lawyer when he is introduced into the novel, and he becomes a serious one by learning to put together the little pieces of evidence he has found, as Hartwright puts together the evidences of his various narrators. As the book closes, the reader learns that Robert "is a rising man upon the home circuit," has transferred his passionate fondness for his friend to marriage to his friend's beautiful sister, and "wondered how [the world] could ever have seemed such a dull, neutral tinted universe" (p. 441). It all sounds very Victorian, very much in line with the *Bildung* narrative.

Robert rescues the world from the disorder that Lady Audley brought into it, banishes her, and re-establishes the traditional order, but as a professional man rather than as an aristocrat. The lawyer inherits the earth.

But these summaries, emphasizing the *Bildung*, distort even as they accurately represent important aspects of the books. Of course, sensation novels are not conventional *Bildungsromane*. Sensation novels are far more interested in the intrigue and detection and disruption than they are in the character of the rescuing professional man, but it is critical to our understanding of the sensation novel that the regular presence of the *Bildung* narrative be noticed. For, as Thomas has said, the stories of the rescuing men, Hartwright, Robert Audley, or Franklin Blake (of *The Moonstone*), for example, are stories of the shift of authority and power from a decaying aristocracy to a new professional elite. The *Bildungsroman*'s engagement with the issue of what the young person will do in a world from which traditional class roles and stable identities have been displaced gets a bold and direct answer from the sensation novel: they will become lawyers or doctors; they will establish themselves by developing the tools that allow them to know, and allow them, through knowing, to affirm and establish order, to make the sorts of distinctions, now justly, about rank and place and personal nature that had been made before by inherited tradition.

While Victorian novels are full of satiric or critical treatments of doctors and lawyers, they are very clearly powers whose work and decisions deeply affect almost everyone. The very plot of *Pickwick Papers* gets its edge from the nastiness of the lawyers, Dodson and Fogg. Lawyers emerge everywhere in Victorian fiction, certainly not only in sensation fiction, making determinations that shape the lives of the protagonists. This is true everywhere in Dickens, and very frequently among the other great novelists, who often would consult lawyers, even in the course of their composition of novels, to make sure that the legal matters inside the novels were correctly handled. In the sensation novel, Thomas claims, the "professions . . . act as the critical authorities through whom a person can establish and sustain his or her new identity in society" (p. 492). Lawyers are the figures who best resolve the problems that come about from the new porousness of class distinction, shoring up the weaknesses of the aristocracy or allowing figures, particularly wicked ones, to pry their way in. We remember how *Vanity Fair*'s central plot lines circled around questions of inheritance and transmission of aristocratic lineage, and how Becky came so close to shattering the class barrier. In the sensation novel, the aristocracy's weakness makes it extraordinarily vulnerable – Sir Percival Glyde turns out to be a fake aristocrat, who very nearly gets away with the fraud; Laura Fairlie is almost successfully transformed from an heir into a poor lunatic; Frederic Fairlie is an aesthete with no energy and a feeble neurotic sensibility; in *Lady Audley's Secret*, the plot circles entirely around the "secret," that Lady Audley is no "Lady," after all, but in fact a bigamist, and from the lower classes, and to disguise that fact has seemed to commit murder.

It is striking that Lady Audley achieves her position in the aristocracy along a plot line that echoes back to Richardson's *Pamela* (1840) and the early days of the modern novel – a young beautiful woman from the lower classes is pursued by an aristocrat, so much so that he ends up marrying her. Sir Michael Audley is certainly no Lovelace. The story of his passion for Lucy Graham is perfunctorily told right at the start of the novel. It is the *Pamela* story once more, this time in a reversal that makes the male lover gentle and innocent and the poor girl conniving and dangerous (rather as Fielding interpreted *Pamela* in his *Shamela* [1841]). But the fundamental story of romances that cross the line between classes gets a new life among the Victorians, where changes in economic and social structures were making such crossing not anomalous but virtually necessary, either to sustain the power of the landed aristocracy through new money, or, as in Lucy Graham, Lady Audley's case, to allow a rise from poverty. Lucy's charm and success make possible the scandalous and disruptive bigamy, which threatens to undermine the notion of hereditary aristocracy built on intrinsic class difference. In place of this false and feeble upper class, the aspiring young *Bildung* heroes assert their authority and claim their fair "Lady." The difference here between the mainstream novel and the sensation novel is not at all "thematic." *Pamela*'s story re-emerges everywhere in the nineteenth-century English novel (in *Jane Eyre* itself, most obviously).[13] After all, to point to only two of the more famous examples, there is a parallel situation in *Bleak House*, with Lady Dedlock already the mother of the illegitimate heroine of the novel. In Hardy's *Tess of the D'Urbervilles* (1891), Alex Durbervilles is not a Durberville; Tess Durbeyfield is a Durberville. In the sensation novel, the unwinding of the intrigues and falsification and the establishment of the right authority are dependent not so much on the intrinsic qualities of the characters but on the skills of the professionals, particularly the lawyer/detectives.

Thus, the sensation novel made part of its appeal to a distinct culture-wide sense that social hierarchies were deeply threatened, and by the emergence of a new class, the professionals, who would be able to establish order and justice by way of legal and detective skills rather than by undisputed heredity. And this entailed a change in emphasis within novels, from the exploration of the complex and mixed evolution of character that marked the best of the Victorian mainstream novels, to elaborate study of how identity is established in the first place. What matters, for example, in the *Middlemarch* story of the banker Bulstrode is not so much the sensation story of his frauds and deceptions – although of course they are indispensable to George Eliot's plot – but the psychology, and the social and ethical implications of his actions, how other members of the Middlemarch society regard him, how he endures the exposure of his hypocrisy, how his hypocrisy was in a curious and important way sincere, how his wife stands by him, how the blame that falls on him circulates through society and rubs off on other characters, like Lydgate. The "sensation" part of the *Middlemarch* story is all in the service of that ethical preoccupation with the nature of character and of social relations that marks moral-realist work. But in Lady Audley, the exposure of Lady Audley's real identity (and real nature?) is the main focus – how she manages her deceptions and how Robert Audley, step by nerve-wracking step, gathers the evidence to expose her. For the sensation novel, as Jonathan Loesberg has argued, the question of identity was as critical as it was for mainstream fiction, but the crucial difference was that the "sensation novel sees the problem in its legal and class aspects rather than in its psychological aspect."[14] And of course, it is the professional who establishes that legal aspect and who, in the end, controls identity itself.

Just the kinds of events that in mainstream realist novels seem contrived and out of harmony with the rest of the novel are the focus and delight (and thrilling shudder) of sensation novels. The ultimate treatment of Lady Audley, her exile to a madhouse and her death, is handled perfunctorily, as are the consequences of the exposure. One important critique of Mrs. Braddon's handling of the matter that recent attentive readers have emphasized is that Lady Audley is too easily condemned as mad, her actions too easily explained as the consequence of her madness. In the course of the novel, it would seem that she is anything but mad. She knows what she wants and she knows what she is doing and she manages to win the affection of virtually everyone with whom she comes in contact. That she confesses to being mad allows Braddon (and Robert Audley) to get rid of her quickly by sending her off to die in the madhouse, with virtually no attention to the horror and injustice of that act, which may be the cruelest thing done in the book. But the act, an authoritarian move by the protagonist/lawyer Robert Audley, re-establishes order both in the novel as novel and in the society. It does so, however, at a price that modern feminist critics in particular quite rightly regard as deeply unjust and inhumane.

And it does so by turning "character" and psychological depth into a figure driven by an inherited disease. The interesting and clever woman is transformed by this kind of professional judgment into a sort of automaton driven by organic forces over which she has no control.

In *The Woman in White* the focus is on the intrigue, and the fiendish and charming brilliance of Count Fosco in developing it, and then, of course, on whether Laura can be rescued from the madhouse. Critics almost unanimously agreed, however hateful they found the story, that Count Fosco was the book's finest creation – in fact, insofar as Collins escaped the total condemnation of the sensation novelist it was because he demonstrated that he had some of the best qualities of the realist in developing interesting characters. But in both novels, the working out of the narrative, the clarification of identity, all depend on the skills of the new professionals in exposing and correcting the false identities. It is striking that Hartwright's resolution of the problems with Fosco have nothing to do with the money that Fosco has won by his contrivances, but with re-establishing the identity of Laura Fairlie.

While the sensation novel does seem much concerned with the new precariousness of identity (related, without question, to the new instability of the new ferociously capitalist society), it is also, as Thomas points out, deeply concerned with money. But this does not make it much of an exception to the Victorian rule. Preoccupation with money, we have seen, was one of the notable characteristics of the Victorian novel as a whole. Money drives characters and shapes characters, but it is clear that its centrality not only represents a culture-wide concern in a newly expanding capitalist society, but also a pervasive unease about it on the part both of the society – struggling to retain its fundamentally Christian ideals – and of the novelists. For lurking around the edges of many realist novels is the realization that while money is essential in the society (and is a crucial element that prods the writers themselves into writing), it is a powerfully corrupting force. To acquire it one must almost inevitably commit oneself to making a serious moral compromise.

The unease extends even into the heart of the sensation novel. No true protagonist in Victorian fiction can be shown acting only for the sake of money, or even acting in part for the sake of money; this is true as well for sensation protagonists. Hartwright, for example, is not successful in money matters; Audley already has money and shows no particular inclination to seek more. The mystery to be solved in sensation novels is likely to be about efforts to acquire money. The climax is the exposure of the effort and its punishment. The same sort of dynamic that works in the mainstream novel seems to be at work in the sensation novel. On the other hand, the virtuous (who usually have the money to start with) are interested in other things – most particularly, of course, in love. (It is striking how *The Moonstone* manages to be about an object of enormous value, although both parties contending for it want it for other than pecuniary reasons. The plot is partly resolved just because a mercenary, not insignificantly an evangelical preacher, becomes the intermediary in the theft of the moonstone, and for him, it matters only in its potential for wealth.)

The wicked seek money. Collins twists the point even further with Fosco because he is not even punished for seeking money. In fact, he does not have to surrender it. This is another disruptive aspect to *The Woman in White*: the wicked seem not to have to pay for their crimes. Fosco in the end, of course, does pay, but it is through a contrivance of plot that has nothing to do with the crime itself. Collins is constrained (whether he wanted it or not) by the conventions of his moment to make Fosco pay. Note how cleverly Collins maneuvers this tricky moral situation at the point in the plot at which Hartwright has forced Fosco to agree to give him the evidence of Laura's identity:

> The one question to consider was, whether I was justified, or not, in possessing myself of the means of establishing Laura's identity, as the cost of allowing the scoundrel who had robbed her of it to escape me with impunity. I knew that the move of securing the just recognition of my wife in the birthplace from which she had been driven out as an impostor, and of publicly erasing the lie that still profaned her mother's tombstone, was far purer in its freedom from all taint of evil passion, than the vindictive motive which had mingled itself with my purpose from the first. . . . I forced myself to make the sacrifice. In plainer words, I determined to be guided by the one higher motive of which I was certain, the motive of serving the cause of Laura and the cause of Truth.[15]

What is particularly fascinating about this twist of the plot is that it affirms that despite all Hartwright has been able to do, the problem of justice is outside human hands – "the work of retribution" is not a human job. Although the implication might seem to be that there is some higher force at work, there is another and stronger one, simply that human intelligence, design, and even passion are subject to inhuman forces.

There is no mention of money here, but Hartwright is determined to act in "freedom from all taint." Vengeance is a tainted motive. The desire for money is a tainted motive. Only the desire for "truth," the dominant value affirmed in novel after Victorian novel, is "untainted." Once truth is established, all else can follow, and so Hartwright's effort to restore Laura's identity is freed from any local desire: the object is truth. And all this is consistent with the almost obsessive empiricism of the narrative method. No opinions allowed. No inferences. No human interference beyond what the human, as an instrument of knowledge, can know first hand, empirically.

The possibility of remaining untainted is connected with the possibility of knowing objectively – or at least empirically. The brilliant Fosco, who knows almost everything, in fact virtually wins. He is defeated only by an accident which, by and large, is inconsistent with Collins' method and style in *The Woman in White*. Collins' imagination, or literary ambition, is constrained by the moral conventions that govern the Victorian novel's relation to money. Indispensable as money is for a decent life, the dominant moral convention requires that novelists minimize the importance of money to their protagonists. Within this moral scheme Fosco must pay the price of plotting to acquire money.

Another striking element of *The Woman in White* here has strong analogues in mainstream fiction. The question is how, given Fosco's remarkable intellectual powers and his charm, can he be made to pay the price that the moral constraints of Victorian culture require. Here the sensation novel threatens to break through those constraints in what would have been a thoroughly shocking way: Fosco would have kept the money and lived happily ever after. To make sure that this doesn't happen, Collins has to shift his narrative strategies and bring into the book the kind of contrivance that seems at last to break down his enormously successful device of keeping even the most extreme events within the limits of representing what seems quite ordinary and realistic life that Mrs. Oliphant was right in seeing as his particular strength. Fosco's plot works. Hartwright, though he has figured it out, is thwarted.

But at this point Collins manipulates events so as to introduce the elaborate story of a great international cabal that has almost nothing to do with the main story. Fosco dies not because Hartwright has figured out how to stop him but because the cabal, finding Fosco through Pesca (who was, it turns out, also involved in the cabal), kills him. The justice Hartwright refused to pursue so as to remain untainted is achieved by forces beyond his control and in fact beyond the range of the realist novel itself, and even of the sensation novel as Collins conceived it. Of course, such twists further enhanced the view of the sensation novel as devoted to the representation of excess and immorality.

But here the sensation novel has only run into just the kind of trouble that mainstream Victorian fiction had to face with some regularity: there seems no way to expose and defeat Fosco without bringing in material outside the norms of the novels they inhabit. Again, the whole Bulstrode plot in *Middlemarch*, however brilliantly theorized by George Eliot, is a case in point. Nemesis enters to wreak its revenge on the hypocritical Bulstrode by the way of chance events that lie well beyond the limits of the intricately realist representations that dominate the book. To restore some kind of order to its mixed, compromised, realist world, George Eliot must push the *Middlemarch* story well beyond Middlemarch and beyond its own ostensible artistic limits.

With all its elaborate plotting, *The Woman in White*, too, must plot beyond its own limits in order to defeat the figure who is smart enough to manipulate the new instabilities of modern Victorian culture. One way to put this almost paradoxical conclusion is that the realist element to which Collins was committed in the writing of this "sensation novel," as it was called, finally must give way to manipulations that seem sensational in order for Collins to be able to reaffirm the basic values of realist domestic fiction. In this respect, *The Woman in White*, even as it produces the conventional ending and restores order and appropriate identity, is at its most subversive. The implication is that while the scandalous and the monstrous can inhabit the everyday world of modern bourgeois society, the means by which that monstrous can be countered must come from outside that everyday world, which thus comes to seem immensely vulnerable, immensely threatened.[16]

III

The whole idea of "sensation fiction," a "form" invented not by the writers but by the critics, who responded negatively to a trend toward violence and excited plotting, pretty much expired by the 1870s. But as a foil against which to understand the complexities of the Victorian novel it remains of particular interest. Its scandalous and transgressive subjects are its obvious identifying marks, but its ways of dealing menacingly with class, money, and identity, staples of the mainstream Victorian novel, help illuminate the strategies and values of the Victorian novel more generally. The sensation novel, insofar as it can be safely identified, is most striking in its difference from the Victorian norm primarily in how easily (or perhaps with what strenuousness) it separates action and knowledge from moral significance. In doing so, it threatens the very idea of stable identity, and with it, the stability of the moral norms and the heavy load of moral responsibility that governed Victorian culture and literature. The connection between knowledge, action, and ethics was always very strong in the Victorian novel. Relying strongly on new ideas out of science and modern psychology, the sensation novel takes dominant Victorian themes to extremes.

In sensation fiction the mind and spirit's dependence on the body tends to be stressed, and in ways that veer far off the Victorian norm, where such matters are also often confronted.[17] Philosophically, the problem created by the unconscious pressures of the body (or society, or any "external" force) is the problem of determinism. And determinism was a conception that worried the Victorians, consciously and philosophically, personally and psychologically. Determinism means that every event, every action, every thought follows as a consequence of previous events. Every effect has a cause. It was an idea indispensable to Victorian science, but it has obvious ethical implications. If everything is determined, including our very thoughts, how can we be held responsible, ethically, for our actions? Determinism seemed to undermine ethics.[18] Of course, very little Victorian fiction – except perhaps George Eliot's – determined to address this issue directly, though it was implicit in the writing of every narrative. Realism is a mode that establishes its authority by dramatizing how events follow each other in causal – and plausible and probable – sequence. Probability in narrative depends on the plausibility of the connection between one event and another.

In sensation fiction, as Thomas has shown, there is a strong emphasis on the body's power to cause behavior that had traditionally been attributed to the workings of the mind as an intelligent, willing, and choice-making force. Identity becomes a physiological as much as a mental thing in sensation fiction, and hence the importance of professionals able to determine

119

material conditions, and biological inheritance. To what degree is our identity established by our conscious will and our imaginations and intellectual qualities? To what degree is it established by our physical nature? Insofar as the physical nature is dominant, the self is in effect at the mercy of biological, not ethical forces. And in novel after sensation novel one finds the body working precisely against personal will. Adjudication of personal identity and personal responsibility passes from the hands of the moral agents into the hands of professionals, particularly doctors who understand the workings of humans as material, biological entities, and the lawyers who interpret the cultural significance of the facts.

Perhaps the most famous (and successful) dramatization of the problem comes in *The Moonstone*, a narrative in which we find the *Bildung* protagonist, Franklin Blake, investigating with the most unfeigned seriousness a crime that he himself had committed. The great puzzle of the novel is just how it is possible for Blake to be the criminal and yet not be responsible for the crime. I remember wondering when I first read the book how Collins was going to get out of this inextricable difficulty. In the course of most of the narrative, the puzzle for readers is why the obvious good girl and heroine Rachel Verinder so distrusts the man she self-evidently loves – the *Bildung* protagonist of the novel. It is a crisis not only of this particular romance but of empiricism itself: can the evidence of the senses – Rachel actually having seen Franklin take the moonstone – be wrong? This kind of problem reverberates well beyond the confines of *The Moonstone*, challenging the very philosophical basis of realist practice.

The solution, however, is entirely physical, and very scientific – or at least made by Collins to feel very scientific. Blake has indeed committed the crime, but under the influence of drugs that leave him entirely unconscious of what he has done. The strange scientist, Ezra Jennings, himself a victim of the drug use that affected Blake, attempts to reproduce the conditions of the "crime" absolutely. He argues that the experiment can work only if those conditions, all of which are physical, can be reproduced. One of the conditions that makes an experiment "scientific," according to some definitions, is that it be reproducible. Collins – and Jennings – are fully aware of the new physiological psychology that might have sanctioned the "experiment."[19] With the focus on the material/scientific explanation of what seems a moral problem, Collins in effect disentangles events from their apparent moral significance – Blake has stolen the jewel, and he is innocent. The realist kind of exploration of the psychology of characters gets translated here into a scientific experiment in which the psychology tells us very little about the nature of the character, but a great deal about the property of drugs.

Thus, while all of these things are reconciled finally to the usual Victorian ethical ordering and to the protagonist's ultimate marriage to the heroine, the gesture of separating action from responsibility has enormous significance. It undercuts the realist attention to the subtle workings of character developing through experience, and it is precisely the reverse of the ethic of moral realism that George Eliot articulated best for her time. In a letter to a good friend, George Eliot wrote, "Every fresh morning is an opportunity that one can look forward to for exerting one's will. I shall not be satisfied with your philosophy till you have conciliated necessitarianism . . . with the practice of willing strongly, of willing to will strongly, and so on, that being what you certainly can do and have done about a great many things in life."[20]

George Eliot's novels consistently dramatize the way in which characters yield to temptation, but her treatment of that surrender to bodily commands always keeps the moral implications of action in the forefront. So in *Adam Bede*, Arthur Donnithorne tries to excuse his adultery with Hetty arguing that, "We may determine not to gather any cherries, and keep our hands in our pockets, but we can't prevent our mouths from watering."[21] For Adam, this is no excuse at all. One must will the body to control itself. Here the physiology is to be dominated by the will, a condition that is completely undercut by the drugs at work on Franklin Blake in *The Moonstone*. Where George Eliot works to reconcile determinism to ethical judgment, Collins in effect denies the possibility, even though, in the working out of his narrative, he reinstates the order that, by implication, cannot be depended on in a world in which psychology is dominated by physiology. *The Moonstone* is built on a "deed" that has no ethical implications at all. It can be and is explained medically even as the explanation divorces action from moral consequence. Of all the aspects of sensation fiction that threaten disruption of established order, that exacerbate cultural anxiety about the instability of class identity, that even threaten firm gender distinctions, the attempt to explain human behavior in strictly physical terms is perhaps the most threatening.

It is fair to say that while the sensation novel had its great moment of popularity in the 1860s, it is most interesting retrospectively as it implies a significant commentary on the dominant conventions of the great tradition of Victorian fiction. It is easy to detect the similarities between mainstream and sensation fiction. Those similarities imply a continuity of cultural concern with the questions of class, identity, and ethics that in various ways trouble virtually all Victorian novels. The *Bildung* tradition is reread in the sensation novel, not because the question of vocation and (moral) action is any less important, but because that very question troubles the culture's sense of stability. The *Bildung* form almost invariably raises questions of class and implies class permeability, and while the realist novel (in its earlier stages at least) tends toward a comic form in which questions of class and romance are reconciled, usually in marriage between hero and heroine, there is nothing inevitable about that development. Indeed, in the later part of the century, the comic form of reconciliation tends to give way to more tragic tendencies, as most famously in Thomas Hardy's novels, but one can see the movement already in George Eliot's work.

And the *Bildung* form itself is challenged in the sensation novel, in part by its continuing preoccupation with identity, by the ease with which people can falsify identity, break through class boundaries, and disrupt the very nature of the self. In a culture in which money has unequivocally replaced class standing as a source of power, protagonists are educated by their experience among the confusions of identity and falsification. The protagonists become professionals, people who acquire new authority in such a society, in particular because they are capable of legally affirming the identity of other characters. They do it by accumulating material evidence that will establish the physical facts essential to selfhood in the sensation novel – and, perhaps, in modern society itself. Along the way, however, even as it relies very heavily on what might be thought of as "scientific method," the sensation novel puts to the test and complicates the Victorian commitment to the empirical. The sensation novel, particularly in Collins' hands, calls into question the epistemological authority that the omniscient narrator of most Victorian novels implies. It turns out that even the evidence of the senses is not entirely reliable.

And thus, however compromised the conclusions to these novels may be, however much they attempt to reconcile the recognition that the monstrous lies beneath the surface of the ordinary with the practical accommodation to reality that the realist novel regularly dramatized, they barely control the deeply disruptive readings of experience that mark the sensation novel and that alert us, as readers, to the threatening and often repressed problems that underlie almost all mainstream Victorian realist fiction.

Notes

1 Ronald Thomas has argued that the "sensation novel" is in certain senses entirely the product of critics who invented the name and condemned the phenomenon. See Ronald Thomas, "The Sensation Novel," in John Richetti, ed., *The Columbia History of the British Novel* (New York: Columbia University Press, 1994), pp. 479–507.

2 Wilkie Collins, *The Woman in White* (Garden City: Dolphin Books, 1977; 1861), ch. 1, p. 15.

3 James's writings about the novel form are voluminous and indispensable to anyone interested in the development of the novel through the nineteenth and into the twentieth century. The prefaces are always interesting. Here is a relatively early formulation from his *The Art of Fiction*: "There are bad novels and there are good novels, as there are bad pictures and good pictures; but that is the only distinction in which I see any meaning, and I can as little imagine speaking of a novel of character as I can imagine speaking of a picture of character. When one says picture one says of character, when one says novel one says of incident, and the terms may be transposed at will. What is character but the determination of incident? What is incident but the illustration of character? What is either a picture or a novel that is *not* of character?" For a valuable collection of James's essays on fiction, see William Veeder and Susan M. Griffin, eds., *The Art of Criticism: Henry James on the Theory and the Practice of Fiction* (Chicago: University of Chicago Press, 1986). This quotation is from p. 174.

4 Anthony Trollope, *An Autobiography* (Oxford: Oxford University Press, 1950; 1883).

5 George Levine, *The Realistic Imagination: English Fiction from Frankenstein to Lady Chatterley* (Chicago: University of Chicago Press, 1981); Gilbert and Gubar, in *The Madwoman in the Attic: The Woman Writer and the Nineteenth-Century Literary Imagination* (New Haven: Yale University Press, 1978), find a similar kind of wildness underlying conventional realism, but they of course find a madwoman in the attic. She is there, but she is in the drawing room, too, as we can see clearly in *Lady Audley's Secret*, another candidate for first sensation novel.

6 Mrs. Oliphant, "Sensation Novels," reprinted in *Wilkie Collins: The Critical Heritage*, ed. Norman Page (London: Routledge and Kegan Paul, 1974), p. 112.

7 Quoted in Page, *Wilkie Collins: The Critical Heritage*, p. 122.

8 Thomas, "The Sensation Novel," p. 482.

9 It is worth noting here that Mrs. Oliphant, an accomplished novelist in her own right, seems to have been swept up by the sensation vogue herself in her excellent novel, *Salem Chapel* (1863). That novel, which focuses primarily on the philosophical and religious problems of Arthur Vincent as he struggles with his barely educated middle-class new parishioners and his attraction (above their class and his) to a beautiful and sympathetic aristocratic woman, suddenly swerves to a sensation plot, whose relation to the whole seems very thin indeed. The villain,

Colonel Mildmay, threatening the well-being of Arthur's sister, occupies rather a lot of Arthur's attention. He, like other sensation protagonists, must turn detective as well. But the resolution of the melodramatic Mildmay plot is not at all what *Salem Chapel* is about. That Mrs. Oliphant, to the bone a domestic realist, should have fallen back on it for the sake of gaining readers, suggests how pervasive and intense the craze for sensation was in the 1860s. But it also might suggest how realism as well as sensationalism was worrying the same problems, in particular, the problems of establishing identity through work, upward class mobility, and money.

10　Wilkie Collins, *The Moonstone* (Oxford: Oxford University Press, 1999), ch. 5, p. 33.

11　It is striking that the most famous detective stories of the century, the Sherlock Holmes stories, were virtually obsessed with the empire, and found its working everywhere, not only in the urban landscape where Holmes was most at home.

12　Mary Elizabeth Braddon, *Lady Audley's Secret* (Oxford: Oxford University Press, 1987), I, ch. 4, p. 32.

13　For a classic discussion of the influence of the *Pamela* story on later fiction, see Robert Palfrey Utter and Gwendolyn Bridges Needham, *Pamela's Daughters* (New York: Macmillan, 1936).

14　Jonathan Loesberg, "The Ideology of Narrative Form in Sensation Fiction," *Representations*, No. 13 (Winter, 1986), p. 117.

15　Collins, *The Woman in White*, Harwrights's Story Continued, ch. 6, p. 523.

16　Loesberg neatly summarizes the complicated implications of the working out of plots in sensation novels, plots that seem to move inexorably toward the revelations necessary to reproduce the threatened order: "the sense of an inevitably mounting sequence is more commonly justified by two other thematic explanations of structure. In one the plot as a whole may be seen as the result of a providential design . . . with the added implication that only such a design could explain the complex comings together of a sensation plot. Another explanation appeals to the empirical sense of the interrelatedness of all facts through the workings of the laws of nature, thus making any crime or conspiracy, no matter how complex, lead to its own uncovering because the very act of veiling through a lie is itself an act connecting with and leading to the facts it intends to hide" ("The Ideology of Narrative Form," p. 126). These two explanations are contradictory, and they are common as well in mainstream fiction. Both emphasize the "inevitability" of the developments and outcome.

17　George Eliot's repeated concern with disciplining the desires to habit in order to keep the instinctive from dominating rational and ethical choice is one form of this emphasis. Hardy's novels are full of figures who seem fated to certain kinds of actions – Henchard, most obviously, but also Tess herself, whose decadent aristocratic look is often alluded to. Victorian novels are also full of compulsive, irrational behaviors that can't be explained in simple ethical terms as failure of will or intention: it is clear enough in *Wuthering Heights*, but even in a novel like Trollope's *He Knew He Was Right*, in which Louis Trevelyan doggedly resists all reasonable explanations and seems half mad, one finds similar behavior. Forces beyond those that would constitute clear moral choice are very often at work in Victorian fiction, but never moreso than in sensation novels.

18　John Stuart Mill realized how essential some resolution to the question of free will and determinism would be if he were to establish the authority of science in matters of morality. His object was to extend science into the study of the human. The famous sixth book of his *System of Logic* (1842) was directly concerned to clarify the problem and argue for the possibility of the reconciliation of scientific determinism with the understanding of human behavior.

19　For a good brief discussion of the science, see John Sutherland's introduction to the Oxford edition of *The Moonstone*, in particular pp. xxv–xxix.

20　*The George Eliot Letters*, ed. G. S. Haight (New Haven: Yale University Press, 1954), vol. 6, p. 66. For a discussion of George Eliot's complicated ideas about determinism, see George Levine, "Determinism and Responsibility in the Works of George Eliot," *PMLA* (June, 1962), pp. 268–79.

21　*Adam Bede*, ch. 16.

Chapter 6

Middlemarch

I

There is no more Victorian novel than *Middlemarch*. If one has learned to read it, one is likely to be at home almost anywhere in the canon of Victorian fiction. And if one reads it well, one will discover how little the "Victorian novel" fits the comfortable and slightly condescending sense of it so widely shared by those who know it best through film versions and who settle for conventional conceptions of "Victorian." *Middlemarch* achieves its representativeness, however, by being unique, immediately recognizable as special even among the very best Victorian novels, like *Bleak House*, for example, or *Vanity Fair*, or *Jane Eyre*, or *Barchester Towers*. As Bach can be taken to be the most baroque of composers because he used and developed the styles of baroque music more richly and fully than any composer before him, so George Eliot, particularly in *Middlemarch*, can be seen as the culmination of the great tradition of moral realism that marked the mainstream of Victorian fiction. She was both theorist and practitioner. Granted that there is an enormous variety inside the label "Victorian," so that no one writer, no one book can possibly synthesize all that diversity, if one wants to get a solid sense of what it means to read a Victorian novel, *Middlemarch* is certainly an excellent place to start.

It's not necessary to claim that *Middlemarch* is the greatest of Victorian novels, although virtually nobody would contest that it is among the greatest. Of all the Victorian writers it is probably Dickens, not George Eliot, who was most richly endowed with genius and whose work is best known and best loved. A careful reading of *Bleak House* might do as much to help our understanding of how to read a Victorian novel as a reading of *Middlemarch*. But *Middlemarch* is not only a great novel; it includes within itself the most serious reflections on the problems of narrative, and works the tradition of Victorian moral realism so far as to bend if not to break it.

In *Middlemarch*, virtually every recurring preoccupation of Victorian fiction is engaged. It is a historical novel, though by indirection, and it is pervasively concerned with how (and in what degree) history and society shape character. It juxtaposes generations and historical moments as Walter Scott had taught the Victorians to do, leaning back for its subject to a generation before the book was actually written and anticipating the modern in its oblique treatment of a great historical moment – the passage of the First Reform Bill in 1832. Thus it looks back to Scott and forward to Henry James, back toward pre-industrial times and forward to a cosmopolitan culture and modernism. It is a psychological novel, bringing the devices by which novelists explore the consciousness of their characters to their fullest development among the Victorians. It is a novel that works within the *Bildung* tradition and yet experiments with it, offering several different ones, both male and female, and managing both to echo the traditional ones, like *Jane Eyre* and *David Copperfield*, and alter them. Like most Victorian novels, it is most particularly engaged with questions of money, class, inheritance, and work, but subjects them all to the play of chance. The familiar Victorian question, "What can I do?" echoes through its pages, relevant to its female protagonists even more than to the men seeking a way to make a living. It thus raises, along its complex pathways, fundamental questions about the condition of women and about the consequences, biographical and social, of their cultural secondariness. It even includes important elements of the sensation novel, and flirts with sensation on its margins despite its insistence on the primacy of the ordinary and the everyday, and it suggests, like the sensation novel, how central to the major concerns of the time was the emergence of the professional (in this case, in particular, the doctor) as an arbiter of identity and a determiner of personal fates.

In furthering the great romantic imagination of the organic connectedness of all things, it becomes one of those characteristic Victorian creations, a multiplot novel,[1] combining intense exploration of individual consciousnesses with similarly intense exploration of social interaction, weaving ostensibly independent stories into a coherent narrative in which every story comments on and influences the others. It employs the dominant narrative method of Victorian realism, the omniscient author convention, but at the same time brings to new levels of sophistication and dramatic intensity the technique of free indirect discourse. And finally (for the moment) it implies the limits of its own method, reminding itself and the reader at every instant that every point of view is limited, that every vision is constrained by the limits of the self that is seeing and by the limits of the moment and the place.

So *Middlemarch* is one of those genuinely encyclopedic novels, like *Don Quixote* or Joyce's *Ulysses*, that seems to incorporate into its narration elements of the whole society and culture from which it has emerged and implicitly makes of its story an exploration of the possibilities of storytelling itself. The moral complexity must be reflected in its epistemological complexity. It dramatizes the novelist's epistemological problem – how to know and represent fully the nature of her characters – as the moral problem of how each character's enclosure in self obscures the reality of the others. Intense look at one character, or adoption of one character's point of view, implies both intellectual and moral blindness.

And this problem is exacerbated by the nature of the book's great enterprise. It is, as the subtitle claims, not merely the story of a single character or of a small set of characters, but *A Study of Provincial Life*. That title itself has rich implications – "study" is a word that alludes to painting as much as it does to scholarship, and tends to undercut the commitment to story and plot so strongly advanced by Wilkie Collins; and "provincial" implies an insistent sense of its opposite, of a more cosmopolitan way of life that is displacing traditional and insular culture through more rapid movement (the new railways figure importantly, if only on the narrative margins of the story), through changes in the financial structures, through international trade and, of course, through expanding awareness of other cultures. For a novel about the provinces, about the "middle" of things, it contains a surprisingly wide range of reference (news of Reform and London politics in general; the building of the railways; the allusions to medical advances on the continent; the discussion of European art, ancient and modern, for example).

Although through much of George Eliot's writing career, exile from the community is almost the worst possible punishment – consider Arthur Donnithorne's fate and Hetty Sorrel's – in *Middlemarch* the narrowness of the community precludes satisfactory absorption of the moral energies of Dorothea, who is ultimately exiled to make her good life in the cosmopolis, not the provinces. There are a surprising number of outsiders among the dramatis personae – Ladislaw, whom many in town suspect of being a

Jew; Casaubon himself, who moves into the area at the start of the book; Bulstrode, the city man, who sets up as banker to find a new life in *Middlemarch*; Lydgate, the aristocratic outsider who sees the town as an excellent place to develop in relative serenity his medical research; Joshua Rigg, to whom Featherstone leaves his estate; and then Raffles, whose efforts at blackmail end by ruining Bulstrode, Lydgate, and himself as well.

The life beyond the limits of provincial Middlemarch is there in the secret lives of many of the characters and, in its sophistication and modernity, echoes through the voice of the narrator. The "Study" sends out tendrils far into the non-provincial elements of the culture, although the work of empire, so important as the context for much ostensibly provincial Victorian fiction, lies very much on the far margins of this novel;[2] the tendrils do, however, snake their way into the network of economic developments in urban society, into national politics and large social changes, into the developments in the arts, but most particularly in science and medicine on the continent and in England. Moreover, *Middlemarch* carefully measures its movements against the rhythms of that major national event, the passage of the First Reform Bill.[3]

Since *Middlemarch* is the most unconventional of conventional novels, it is both an excellent representative of the Victorian novel and a critique of its conventions because of the creative and original way it plays with them. Watching it at work will do much to demonstrate how inadequate to real encounters with Victorian fiction our conventional and comfortable sense of that form is, and what a rich, strange, difficult, and wonderful thing it can be.

The extensive reading of *Middlemarch* here is designed not to offer some "definitive" reading but to show elements of the Victorian novel considered more generally elsewhere in this book at work in a particular novel. The fundamental characteristics of the Victorian novel to be considered here help establish that "family resemblance" that makes sense of the category "Victorian novel."

"Connectedness" is a key to the very Victorian nature of the book – connectedness of multiple and potentially disparate elements, connectedness that implies an epistemology: what and how can one know when everything can only be known in relation to everything else? Most important, connectedness implies an ethics as well; virtue lies just in the pursuit of connectedness. "I should learn everything then," says Dorothea to herself just at the start of the novel (ch. 3, p. 28).[4] A woman "ardent, theoretic, and intellectually consequent" (ch. 3, p. 29), Dorothea seeks "a binding theory which could bring her own life and doctrine into strict connexion with that amazing past" (ch. 10, p. 84). The ideal is in place for the book itself, even while it (gently) satirizes the absolute impossibility of her moral and intellectual ambition. Her marriage crisis comes upon her on her honeymoon in Rome, where the "broken revelations" of that city's religious and secular past, and the vision of "ruins and basilicas . . . mixed confusedly" and the impossible contrast between the gaudiness of St. Peter's and the rigorous austerity of "English and Swiss Puritanism" and the contrast between her marital ambitions and "the endless minutiae" of her now married life, leave her disenchanted, stunned, and weeping (ch. 20, pp. 191–2).

Dorothea's pain lies in not being able to make connections, though she desires desperately to find them. But many figures in the novel have opposite desires – to separate the parts of their lives. And this is morally (one might add aesthetically) disastrous. The central dramas of the novel, both psychological and social, spin upon the question of coherence. Blocking the past, dividing public from private, mind from body, leads to moral disaster. The highest morality in this narrative lies in the quest, at whatever cost, to make one's individual life both internally coherent and coherent with the community in which it moves. Ethics and epistemology are one in dealing with the questions of how to understand the ultimate entanglement of all things, and how to respond to that entanglement, how to act without hurting others (even, and particularly, those whom one doesn't know) or compromising oneself. One needs to know in order to act rightly; one needs to recognize the extraordinary intricacy and complexity of things in order to know rightly. *Middlemarch*, as it incorporates so much of the Victorian worldview into its narration, dramatizes the impossibility of disentangling and the enormous difficulty of knowing and of acting rightly. "What connection can there be?" That question borrowed here again from *Bleak House* is asked and answered on every page of *Middlemarch*. As with everything else in George Eliot's work, it is ultimately a question about morals, and if in less rigorous and systematic form, it haunts the Victorian novel.

II

Before looking at *Middlemarch* from the inside, it will be useful here to remind ourselves of the material conditions that lay behind the creation of *Middlemarch*. Although the average reader can certainly fully grasp the workings of the book without attention to its publishing history, that history is distinctly relevant to many of the narrative's details, subtle and not so subtle. It is worth noting that *Middlemarch*, like most of the other novels discussed in this book, was also published serially, in parts, but in an unusual way. While the fates of the novel's characters hinge strikingly on the question of money, it is interesting to note to what degree financial considerations influenced its shape and form. By the time of her writing of *Middlemarch*, George Eliot had established herself as a major literary figure. It is true that there had been some complaining that her early work, in *Adam Bede* (1859) and in *The Mill on the Floss* (1860), had not been matched by the novels that followed, except for the small fable-like masterpiece, *Silas Marner* (1861). But that early burst of genius had established George Eliot as a master; whatever she did afterwards commanded attention. It wasn't, however, until *Middlemarch* (1871–2) that she established herself as indisputably the most important living novelist in England (Dickens had died in 1870).

Though a writer who commanded respect and an audience, George Eliot had always been concerned about how much she could earn from her writings. She relied on G. H. Lewes, with whom she had eloped in 1854 and scandalized much of polite society, to do the negotiating and to advise her. None of this, of course, diminishes the utter seriousness of her sense of vocation as a novelist. She was outspokenly hostile to the idea that ambition and commercial success might be the motive for writing, and she believed, as Rosemarie Bodenheimer has forcefully shown, that she had to (and could) justify her writing by offering to her readers new ideas that her audience genuinely needed.[5] She put therefore a great premium on writing originally, and this surely partly accounts for the pain and anguish she seemed to suffer in writing each of her novels. The dedicated seriousness, perhaps overseriousness, of her relation to the writing suggests a tension between profit and art that in other Victorian writers was less pronounced. Writers like Dickens and Thackeray and Trollope worried very little about that tension, assimilating the attempt to attract a large audience and satisfy publishers' demands to their own writing habits. In George Eliot one can watch a very modern tension between sales and art beginning to develop.

For her, mere literary ambition had become identified with economic ambition, ambition unworthy of the calling of art – a moral and an aesthetic calling. She was appalled by what she saw as the commodification of literature going on all around her, and she regarded parts publication with particular distrust. Such publication emphasized the commercial conditions governing writing, and she was convinced that such publication tended to produce inferior art. But she was fully involved in the commerce of art, despite the fact that Lewes did most of the mediating. She herself had switched publishers for what was then a whopping sum of money in 1862 to have *Romola* published in the new literary journal, *Cornhill*. *Middlemarch* also was published in parts, and its publishing history, though governed in part by the exigencies of her creative imagination, reveals a very sharp eye for economic advantage. Lewes bore the burden of making the arrangements. Inside the narrative of *Middlemarch*, as we shall see, there is a constant struggle to disentangle money and ambition from action: it is an almost obsessive preoccupation of the book, as it is also (we have seen) a regular motif of the Victorian novel. There can be little doubt, however, that George Eliot – given the solemnity of her commitment to her vocation – felt directly threatened by just that phenomenon that had become central to the very conception of the sensation novel – that everything, including people, was being transformed into commercial objects, into property and money.

George Eliot began thinking about and sketching a projected novel, to be called "Middlemarch," as early as 1867, though serious writing didn't start until 1869. But in 1870, with "Middlemarch" going slowly, she broke off to write a story called "Miss Brooke." As that story grew and she resumed work on *Middlemarch*, George Eliot came to realize that the "Miss Brooke" story could be woven into the *Middlemarch* story, and one can in fact see the stitching in chapter 10 of the first book, when Dorothea attends a party at which are present Lydgate and other prominent Middlemarch figures. There is a telling moment when Lydgate, seeing Dorothea, thinks, "She is a good creature – that fine girl – but a little too earnest" (p. 91). The one novel comments ironically on the other, as they are joined together (and will climax in the last chapters of the completed novel, as Dorothea comes to Lydgate's aid and justifies her earnestness). *Middlemarch* becomes, then, a multiplot novel, and once the connection is made, the significance of all actions is virtually doubled.

The coupling of the two novels brought practical problems, for George Eliot recognized that the materials she had were far too extensive for the normal formats of Victorian publishing. What began as an aesthetic and a moral choice determined her on a new twist in publishing. She would certainly not publish the book in monthly installments, as she had done with *Romola* in the *Cornhill* and as, in independent publication, Dickens had done. But *Middlemarch* would be too big to be published in the usual "triple decker" format, that is, in the three volumes that were virtually always required by the lending libraries, whose economic power almost totally controlled the literary marketplace.

The new idea was to publish the book in parts after all, although in fewer installments and larger parts than Dickens had done. Although George Eliot preferred to have finished her books completely before publication began, she agreed to this very practical arrangement with her loyal publisher, John Blackwood, and over the course of little more than a year, the parts appeared somewhat irregularly, every one or two months, each the size of one half of each of the novel's eight "books." Publication started in December of 1871 and concluded in December of 1872, but when it started, George Eliot was still only working on Book 4. Each installment was much more substantial than the 32 pages characteristic of Dickens' monthly installments, but then while Dickens' installments cost only one shilling, *Middlemarch*'s cost five shillings. Because it required from its readers a greater investment of time and money, it attracted a different kind of readership. It is no surprise that while *Middlemarch* was a very successful book, it didn't approach in sales or popularity the successes of most of Dickens' work.

Certainly, George Eliot did not bend *Middlemarch* in response to the sales of the first books, as Dickens sometimes did during serial publication of his novels. But parts publication did have some little effect on the arrangement of chapters (George Eliot wanted to avoid allowing some important characters to lapse from the consciousness of her readers because they made no appearance in an installment and wanted as well to be sure that each installment had roughly the same physical thickness).[6] No doubt the installments were much fuller and therefore more flexible than Dickens' monthly publications, but there can be no doubt as well that despite her great freedom to write the book as she wanted, George Eliot felt the pressure of the format as she wrote. It is ironic, then, that this most serious of Victorian writers, the one most self-consciously opposed to the commercialization of fiction and most intensely dedicated to the moral and intellectual purity of her work, produced her greatest book for serial publication. The compromise might well make the moral climax of a realist novel by George Eliot.

III

While *Middlemarch* is indeed a social and encyclopedic novel, it carries on within its multiple narratives the central tradition of realism, which, in its self-conscious rejection of fantasy and ideals, in the mode of *Don Quixote*, is immediately tied to the more modern form, the *Bildungsroman*. Virtually all of the major themes and preoccupations of *Middlemarch* are compatible with this tradition, and fully to grasp what is going on in the novel it is essential that one recognize the presence of the *Bildungsroman* and the particular ways the form is used. It is striking that George Eliot bogged down in writing "Middlemarch" until she saw the possibility of blending "Miss Brooke," her story of Dorothea, with the larger one. Although Dorothea's story does not start in early childhood, she is nevertheless the perfect *Bildung* protagonist. Innocent, orphaned, misguided by reading and idealism, provincial, misunderstood by the very ordinary people among whom she lives, and insufficiently knowledgeable about herself, Dorothea must come to terms with a reality into which in her ignorance she stumbles badly, and must make her compromises with the hard unaccommodating actual.

She does not begin in hardship, as did David and Jane, but is, rather, a child of privilege. Because she is freer from material constraint than most other *Bildung* protagonists, Dorothea's troubles are of her own making. Her wealth frees her from material constraints and thus her story has some of the quality of romance,[7] allowing the drama to be located almost entirely in consciousness. The problem, however, is still the *Bildung* problem: how does one imagine oneself, how does one conduct oneself without guidance from parents in a culture in which social and political change are everywhere and traditional roles and responses won't do? The critical importance of this problem acquires particular force in *Middlemarch* because its *Bildung* narratives are self-consciously set against the background of the First Reform Bill. National politics enter the personal narratives only by inspiring Mr. Brooke to run for Parliament, and, as a consequence, bringing to town the cosmopolitan outsider, Will Ladislaw (who is also in the process of formation, adrift and aimless, almost like the male protagonists of *Lady Audley's Secret* and *The Moonstone*). But national politics, national political and social change, affect each of the young figures in *Middlemarch*.

Dorothea's narrative follows the main lines of the English *Bildung*, taking her from the provinces to the city and modernity, establishing for her a firm identity, marrying her finally to Ladislaw, who becomes "an ardent public man" ("Finale," p. 819), but leaving her far from the ideal that had been her youthful ambition. The first moral crisis, amidst the "stupendous fragmentariness" (ch. 20, p. 191) of Rome, leaves Dorothea in something like despair. Against the background of a violent and crowded modernity and a fragmentary antiquity, and trapped in a marriage to a husband who uses convention to protect himself from feeling, Dorothea undergoes the first radical step of her *Bildung*.

As a woman, there was nothing she could do that might have helped her fulfill her sense of ideal possibility. Even before Rome, when she first visits her future husband's estate, "she felt some disappointment, of which she was yet ashamed, that there was nothing to do in Lowick" (p. 76). The thought is both comic and entirely serious; she almost wishes that there were suffering on the estate, as there was on her uncle's, so that she could bring in modern improvements to help the tenants. Her plans there for housing are indulged entirely because Sir James Chettam loves her, and are condescended to throughout. Casaubon's request that she commit her life to his papers is merely monstrous, though, given her ideals of submission, she comes within moments of making the commitment.

At the critical moment in Dorothea's narrative, which is also at the crisis of Lydgate's career, Dorothea's answer to the question "What can I do?" takes a local, non-vocational turn and suggests most fully how George Eliot translates the *Bildung* question for women. What she can do is not a vocation but a local intense act of sympathy. Against the common sense of the community, she stands by Lydgate, refusing to believe that he had in effect killed Raffles for Bulstrode by prescribing incorrectly. In chapter 81, which George Eliot thought of as the true climax of the novel, Dorothea, attempting to muffle her own pain at the thought of Rosamond and Will Ladislaw's flirtation, goes to assure Rosamond and in so doing to assist Lydgate. It is a powerful chapter in which, for one moment, Dorothea breaks through the hardened egoism of Rosamond just because of her own extraordinary moral generosity. It is a moment in which Rosamond's story moves to the edge of that growth to maturity that is so central to the *Bildung* narrative, but it remains only a moment, while the event marks an epoch in Dorothea's life, confirming at last the moral power of her often misplaced idealism and trust. Within Dorothea's *Bildung* it is the great moral achievement emerging from her powers to control her own pain. It is, at any rate, what Dorothea can do, and though it is local and not a life's vocation, it opens for her the satisfying life she will lead with Ladislaw.

After that great moment, the novel returns more directly to the practical possibilities of a woman's life in historical context. What she then "does" is assist her husband in the work of reform – she "could have liked nothing better, since wrongs existed, than that her husband should be in the thick of a struggle against them, and that she should give him wifely help" ("Finale," p. 819). In the conclusion George Eliot directly confronts the disappointment that her readers are likely to have felt at the diminution of Dorothea's ambitions: "Many who knew her, thought it a pity that so substantive and rare a creature should have been absorbed into the life of another, and be only known in a certain circle as a wife and a mother." But this is first a *Bildungsroman*, entailing compromise, and second, a woman's *Bildungsroman*, a form that necessarily had to come to terms with the very limited options of what to do that were available to women. Anticipating the novel-readers' complaints, which she knew would be the same as the complaints of those within the book who recognize Dorothea's substantiveness, the narrator counters: "But no one stated exactly what else that was in her power she ought rather to have done." It is the pervasive problem of the Victorian female *Bildungsroman*.

Dorothea's story has none of the fairy-tale quality of Jane Eyre's or David Copperfield's. It is a *Bildung* that threatens to turn from comedy to tragedy, a turn that might be said to happen to the late Victorian novel in general, most famously in the novels of Thomas Hardy. But it is insufficient to read *Middlemarch* as though it were all about Miss Brooke. The novel, like almost all multiplot novels (like, for example, *Vanity Fair*), though yet more intensely, requires that every particular narrative be read in the light of the others. So Dorothea's *Bildung* can only be fully understood in the light of Lydgate's story and Ladislaw's and Fred Vincy's and Mary Garth's. Each narrative, so tightly focused, it would seem, on the individual consciousness of the protagonist, registers the interplay of character with context and with other characters; formally, it gives shape to the diverse stories as each echoes or modifies the others.

Not all the other young protagonists follow the same paths in their pursuit of identity, maturity, and work. Mary Garth undergoes very little real development because she enters the novel almost fully formed (and follows the moral lead of her parents). None of the others move from province to city (unless one counts Ladislaw, a cosmopolitan figure to start with). But to give some idea of how the variations and interconnections work, I want to look very briefly here at two of the alternatives to and commentaries on Dorothea's – the development of Lydgate and of Fred Vincy.

Lydgate is the masculine alternative to Dorothea. In a conventional realist novel, he would certainly have been Dorothea's lover and ultimate husband. The two stories join just at the point when it is too late for that happy romantic resolution (and George Eliot plays heavily on the irony of Lydgate's failure to recognize Dorothea's value, suggesting that he too begins with false romantic ideals, his more banal than Dorothea's and saturated with the conventions of his time). George Eliot's decision to link "Miss Brooke" with *Middlemarch* must surely have been connected to her desire to test out and reject the conventional plot by juxtaposing the *Bildung* stories. Dorothea's story, like Lydgate's, explores the necessity and the possibility of reconciling the public and private life. While such reconciliation is Dorothea's ideal, Lydgate fails even to recognize the problem or to realize how essential it is to his own success and, yet more ironically, how his own scientific theories, followed out, would lead him to the unifying vision that Dorothea longs for. He simply assumes that his private life will be a comforting alternative world when he returns fatigued from his scientific work.

Lydgate's story plays the unreflectingly conventional quality of his personal life against the rigorous and difficult originality of his professional life. While Dorothea and Lydgate make the same mistake, misreading surfaces and mismarrying, Dorothea does it because she is farsighted and can't recognize the quotidian realities before her face – Mr. Casaubon's mole that so appalls Celia, for example, or – more important – the aridity of his character. Lydgate makes those mistakes not because he is seeking a work to do: he knows what he wants to do, and it has deep moral significance. He makes it because while in his research he recognizes the interrelatedness of things, in his life he doesn't. There's an epistemological laziness that is also an ethical laziness. His brilliant vision, laid out in free indirect discourse in chapter 16, leads him in his studies to "that arduous invention which is the very eye of research, provisionally framing its object and correcting it to more and more exactness of relation" (p. 163).

Lydgate's is, in a way, an anti-*Bildung*. He does have many of the typical characteristics of the *Bildung* hero: though of an aristocratic family, he really has no family – something that Rosamond finds out in a costly and painful way. Like David, like Jane, like Will Ladislaw, he strikes out to break free from the past. He denies the aristocratic tradition (about which Rosamond, who reads only conventional literature, fantasizes). But the story opens on him a bit later than for the other *Bildung* protagonists we have encountered because he seems already to have lost his innocence.

After his shattering affair with the actress Laure, he is convinced that "illusions were at an end for him" (ch. 15, p. 152). "The man was still in the making," comments the novel's narrator: "character too is a process and unfolding" (ch. 15, p. 147), and what follows shows that, indeed, his illusions were not at an end, for he is as fooled by Rosamond's beauty as he was by Laure's.

If the English *Bildung* always pushes toward a compromise with the harsh unaccommodating actual, the Lydgate story pushes hard enough to turn compromise into defeat. Dorothea's life moves on in compromise with her larger ideals, but with a sense that those ideals pervade her compromised life. Lydgate's life ends in mere respectability, with no work of consequence. His story is of a kind of devolution, a change backwards, for his illusion about Rosamond guarantees the failure of his ambitions and ideals. He succumbs to his own illusions and "matures" only after it is too late. His "hair never became white," but before he dies he gains an "excellent practice" dealing with rich people's illnesses in Bath. This is precisely Rosamond's ideal, and precisely not his. However outwardly successful he became, "he always regarded himself as a failure" ("Finale," p. 818). The outer shape of his story, then, seems to answer to the *Bildung* prescription – he is wealthy, widely recognized, author of a book on the gout. But the inner shape is quite different: all ideals not only compromised but absolutely thwarted. His early death is the material indication of his failures. Rosamond triumphs.

The "realism" of his story lies particularly in its representation of the other side of *Bildung* – the loss of illusions and the utter moral defeat, under the pressure of daily details, by the ordinary demands and bills and responsibilities of domestic life. In Lydgate's story, George Eliot treats compromise as defeat, while in Dorothea's there is an indication that while forced to compromise, she retains her passion for the ideal and – as the famous conclusion of the novel says – "the effect of her being on those around her was incalculably diffusive." Lydgate's fate, cushioned by wealth and worldly success, anticipates the more extreme defeat of Jude the Obscure. Jude dies an absolute failure, but uncushioned by money or conventional propriety, alone, unfulfilled, having achieved nothing. The difficulty of overcoming contingency and one's own personal limits becomes in Hardy what it is beginning to be in George Eliot, too great to be overcome.

Operating at a lesser level of intensity, but of great importance to the narrative, there is another *Bildung*, that of Fred Vincy. Obviously, George

Eliot imagines Fred as a character without the romantic aspirations of Dorothea or Lydgate. He is deliberately conceived as a very ordinary young man, and yet his fate too is entangled in the history that lies on the margins of the story. He does not think of reform in any way, but he has to learn not to be a Cambridge man and get practical – reforming himself, he learns something about modern farming. His story – disinheritance, practical work done honorably, marriage – embodies in the most everyday terms the historical transition that always lies behind the Victorian *Bildungsroman.*

Although Fred's story is distinctly about his "formation," his "education," it is also true that he doesn't quite fit the description of the normal *Bildung* protagonist. After all, he has both a mother and a father. But they are, to put it a bit crudely, morally useless to him. Fred, because he is expected to inherit Featherstone's wealth and Stone Court, has no ambition for work. He does not ask himself what he can do. But his story, nevertheless, by expelling him from the fantasy world of inheritance and the pre-modern order of things, forces him too to ask that question. In debt to Mary Garth's father, he must find something to do. And as with other *Bildung* protagonists, he finds an alternative to traditional parents, in his case, with Caleb Garth.

So George Eliot plays another variation on the *Bildung* theme and allows it to work out happily. This has partly to do, it seems, with the very unmodern work and way of life Fred adopts, the old-fashioned relationship with a rather old-fashioned Mary. Fred never gets the unearned wealth of inheritance; but it is the perfect *Bildung* ending because the compromise includes marriage to the right woman – not Agnes, "looking upward," but Mary Garth, who clearly is depicted as in every respect, intellectual, practical and moral, Fred's superior. But he actually produces a practically useful book, "Cultivation of Green Crops and the Economy of Cattle-Feeding" ("Finale," p. 816).

These three *Bildung*-type narratives comment on and echo each other as they challenge conventional fictional handlings of the usual boy-girl relationships and the usual youth-to-maturity development. In the society coming on as the major narratives of *Middlemarch* close, there is everywhere the need for the young to learn what they are by learning what they can and should do. It is interesting how, throughout the large panorama of the novel, George Eliot offers only one adequate (perhaps idealized) pair of parents, the Garths. Dorothea has no parents, Lydgate only snobbish relatives; Ladislaw is also an orphan, drifting and without direction.

The Vincys are narrow-minded and thus fail in their moral direction of Fred and Rosamond. Both these young figures are absolutely absorbed in fantasies of inheritance, direct, or through marriage. The Garths are George Eliot's single answer from the values of the past, and it is important to note that Mr. Garth leads Fred into the present and understands how to deal with the railroad, which would change forever the commerce and the social structure of towns like Middlemarch. The basic *Bildung* plot is thus indispensable to the imagination of this world in transition, and, as George Eliot dramatizes, not quite adequate to it.

IV

While the appearance of *Bildung* narratives inside the major realist text of Victorian fiction is not a surprise – the *Bildung* form being, in a way, the ur-form of realism – the appearance of sensation fiction would seem to be. George Eliot was not sympathetic to sensation fiction. Unlike Collins, she did not take it as her first responsibility to tell a story. Her focus, like Trollope's, was on the development of character, and where the sensation novel found its thrills in excesses of action, George Eliot's kind of realism achieves its most intense feelings in the exploration of character and the deep tensions, psychological and moral, that develop internally. The great emotional climaxes of *Middlemarch* come not in the hunt to expose criminality or explain mysteries, or in the crimes themselves, but in intimate moments that make subtle changes in the readers' sense of the characters, as when Mrs. Bulstrode, that "imperfectly-taught woman," goes down to her shamed and defeated husband, and says merely, "Look up, Nicholas." It is one of the great scenes in English literature, and nothing happens:

> They could not yet speak to each other of the shame which she was bearing with him, or of the acts which brought it down on them. His confession was silent, and her promise of faithfulness was silent. Open-minded as she was, she nevertheless shrank from the words which would have expressed their mutual consciousness, as she would have shrunk from flakes of fire. She could not say, "how much is only slander and false suspicion?" and he did not say, "I am innocent." (ch. 74, p. 740)

Similarly, the scene that George Eliot regarded as the climax of the book, Dorothea's interview with Rosamond in chapter 81, itself intense only in the psychological play between the two, culminates when the inveterately self-involved Rosamond, under the emotional shock of Dorothea's great moral generosity, notices that her husband looks as though he has been suffering: "How heavy your eyes are, Tertius," says Rosamond, "and do push your hair back" (ch. 85, p. 787). This is hardly the stuff of sensation, and it depends on a long novel full of fine psychological analysis and subtle moral discriminations.

One might argue that these moments are far more powerful than anything a sensation novel might offer, but that would be beside the point. What matters, for the purposes of this reading, is the literary method here – not directed at developing elaborate plots to elaborate climaxes, as in the experiment that, in *The Moonstone*, dramatizes how Franklin Blake can both be and not be the thief of the moonstone, or as in the confrontation with Fosco near the end of *The Woman in White*. Rather, it depends on a rich understanding of the psychology of the individual characters, even of so minor a character as Mrs. Bulstrode, and on a long-developed interest in their moral dramas.

Nevertheless, the "real" world of *Middlemarch* depends upon the existence of a whole world of chance crossings and scandal and outrageous plotting, of murder, drugs, false identities, gambling, and even illegitimate (if, yes, rather mild) sexuality. *Middlemarch* was written near the end of the decade in which the sensation novel most flourished, but while it is unlikely that the fashion had much to do with George Eliot's subject matter, the conventions of the sensation novel were, as I have tried to show, not so far from those of the mainstream novel as the category "sensation novel" would seem to suggest. Behind the domestic matter and psychological subtleties of all her books there lurked, as noted in chapter five on sensation fiction, a whole series of thoroughly sensational elements – most recently, for her, in *Felix Holt* (1866), where, as Rosemary Ashton points out, "it is striking" that George Eliot "uses the same kind of plot mechanisms of mistaken identity, inheritance, and blackmail as Dickens's and Collins's novels of the early 1860s."[8] It is not generally noted that the far more distinguished and representative *Middlemarch* includes precisely the same elements.[9]

While readers need not know anything about George Eliot's biography to recognize the remarkable powers of *Middlemarch*, it is worth mentioning that behind George Eliot's almost oppressive respectability and intellectual seriousness there lay the life of Mary Ann Evans, which had elements of sensation in it that George Eliot tried very hard to repress. In her early years in London, Mary Ann lived in a ménage á quatre with the publisher John Chapman, his wife, and his mistress. During that time Mary Ann began taking full responsibility for the contents of Chapman's journal, *The Westminster Review*, although all her contributions were anonymous. Whatever the reasons, the wife and mistress joined forces to expel Mary Ann from the house. Later, famously, she and George Henry Lewes, a thoroughly married and brilliant jack-of-all-trades intellectual, eloped together to Europe in 1854, and returned to remain together, unmarried, until Lewes's death in 1878. Some years into the relationship, Mary Ann began writing fiction and took the pen name of George Eliot, remaining in disguise until the appearance of *The Mill on the Floss*. The point here is not the pleasure of gossip, but the fact that George Eliot built her reputation as a sage, as the most respectable of novelists, as the hostess of weekly soirees, on the back of a rather famous scandal, just as her novels, realist almost to the core, build their subtleties often on materials that would be the very heart of sensation fiction.

The limits of Victorian realism, as I have suggested elsewhere, entail the exclusion of grand events, great historic moments, actions of excess – violent, sexual, or criminal – and limit the range of protagonists' ambitions by describing a world so thick with details, so constraining in its power to shape character and identity, that the most noble of figures, even a Dorothea, can never achieve world-historical action – of the sort that figure in the "Prelude" about Saint Theresa. Moreover – an oddity of Victorian realism – it is virtually impossible to represent within its terms a thoroughly villainous villain, someone unequivocally evil, unless it can be shown how the excess is somehow, detail by detail, the product of a long series of small events. George Eliot talks frequently of "necessary sequence," a philosophical conception with deterministic implications, but also a condition of a plausible, realist novel. All conditions are to be explicable only as they follow "inevitably" from earlier ones. It is Darwinian gradualism built into narrative form. But sensation fiction denies that model entirely. And *Middlemarch* is a remarkable example of the way the constraints of the realist imagination need to be violated if the narrative is to be "realistic" in the simpler sense of plausibly representative of the way life works.[10]

Consider the elements of *Middlemarch* that tend to get less attention, except as aberrations, as evidences of some weakness or flaw in George Eliot's powers as a writer and in her realistic imagination. First, and most immediately obvious, there is the whole background narrative of Lydgate's life before he comes to *Middlemarch*. It should be noted that he comes to the little town in the middle (as all things realist seem to aspire to be) with world-historical ambitions. He wants to discover what is "the primitive tissue" (ch. 15, p. 147) and through that discovery to "pierce the obscurity of those minute processes which prepare human misery and joy, those invisible thoroughfares which are the first lurking-places of anguish, mania, and crime, that delicate poise and transition which determine the growth of happy or unhappy consciousness" (p. 163). Clearly Lydgate's work is also the work of the novelist, of George Eliot. And it implies the same paradox of the realist – that is, through the minute, delicate examination of the details of life, the novelists and Lydgate will discover the "lurking-places of anguish, mania, and crime." Realist characters find themselves inside sensation novels. Lydgate's literal past is a "sensation," for the actress he fawns on, follows through Europe, and proposes to, has in fact intentionally killed her husband on stage and feigned accident. Lydgate's discovery of this fact – "I meant to do it" in italics (ch. 15, p. 151) – is the stuff of pure sensation. His formation, his *Bildung*, is to take him, as it is to take the novel he inhabits, out of that world of excess into the constrained world of domesticity, from fantasies of romantic love to the solid reality of the cost of furniture and of domestic constriction.

But even there George Eliot runs into difficulties. As we have seen in chapter three on realism and in discussion of the *Bildungsroman*, one of the dominant themes of Victorian realism is just that point George Eliot makes at the end of *Middlemarch*, that everyone's being is "greatly determined by what lies outside it." It is a lesson in connectedness that Lydgate must learn, and thus the plot of *Middlemarch* is all about entanglements – social, physical, temporal. And it makes clear that Lydgate's "spots of commonness," his vulgar interest in material appearances, doom him to failure in his professional life, where he is not common at all. But the narrative trick is to dramatize the way in which those entanglements cause his fall.

The instrument, by various circuitous and complex means, is Bulstrode, and Bulstrode imports into the plot (along, yet more secretly, with Casaubon, with whom there is a complex distant connection) the elements of the sensation novel. There is no need to disentangle all the complex strands of the connection. What is striking about it is just that it is so complex. To demonstrate that the world is entirely connected in the causal modes of scientific theory, George Eliot must work out a plot as complex as any sensation novel's. The sensation parts of *Middlemarch* would have done Wilkie Collins proud. In the relations among Bulstrode, Ladislaw, and Casaubon, there is the story of intrigue, of illegitimacy, of two generations of deferred inheritance and misidentifications. All of this climaxes and gets revealed with the entrance of Raffles the blackmailer threatening to expose Bulstrode's past.

George Eliot needs all these things to mark for the reader a past that has been artificially disconnected from the present. As Dorothea strives for a vision of the world that integrates everything, so does the novel itself; in effect, it punishes with Nemesis efforts to disguise connections. To do that, it needs to introduce into the novel elements of "sensation," ostensibly incompatible with the realist mode and the intricate psychology of characterization with which George Eliot achieves her greatest and most characteristic successes. Bulstrode moves from his seedy past life in London to a life of the most austere piety in Middlemarch, where nobody knows of his past and his piety does not smack of hypocrisy. He is distinctly vulnerable to blackmail. And it is on Bulstrode that Lydgate becomes dependent for his hospital work and, in the end, his research. Similarly, Ladislaw has been swindled out of his legitimate inheritance by Casaubon's quite deliberate passivity in the work of uncovering the line of parentage and inheritance from which Bulstrode and Casaubon have profited. All of these things are made possible by the other twist of the plot otherwise irrelevant to Bulstrode and Lydgate, that is, the introduction of frog-faced Joshua Rigg as nephew and heir to Mr. Featherstone, and through him Raffles, his step-father/blackmailer, who finds a piece of paper with the name Bulstrode upon it.

When spelled out in detail, this plot is breathtakingly chancy and elaborate – right out of the sensation novel. George Eliot is particularly self-conscious about that, pausing as she tries to explain how it is that Raffles can emerge on the scene as a blackmailer. "Who shall tell what may be the effect of writing," she asks. It is difficult not to connect "writing" here not only to the paper that Raffles has found, but to the novel itself, narrating ramifying connections, aspiring to ramifying connections. Writing, says the narrator, "may end by letting us into the secret of usurpations and other scandals gossiped about long empires ago: – this world being apparently a huge whispering-gallery" (ch. 41, p. 406).

We have seen how, in the sensation novel, there is usually a protagonist who, in the mode of professional lawyer or detective, works through the seemingly impossible complications of plot, and, by way of his investigation, is in a position to establish the identity or expose the false identity of the main figures in the novel. There is not quite such a figure in *Middlemarch*, although it is clear from the handling of Featherstone's will, and from the obscure and difficult tracing of Ladislaw's inheritance, that in *Middlemarch* as in the sensation novels, professional authority is required to establish identity. Or, to put it differently, the dominant plots in *Middlemarch* are designed to resist this professionalization, this mode of establishing identity regardless of intrinsic qualities of character. The sensation plot threatens character, both technically, in the way it unfolds and attracts attention, and morally, within the narrative, as it falsifies or authorizes regardless of merit.

Mary Garth must labor to sustain her integrity, with Featherstone in particular, regardless of the scrutiny to which she would be subjected. Rosamond struggles to establish her identity as within the aristocratic family from which her husband comes, while Lydgate struggles – himself a professional – to affirm his own independent identity. The Garths as a family are deeply resistant to the elements of the novel that belong to the sensation narrative. They will not allow the slightest taint on their integrity and are not at all tempted by money. But the "whispering gallery" that is the world of the novel makes that kind of exemption from blame, from false identification, extremely difficult, and sustains its surveillance over everyone.[11] *Middlemarch* might be described as a novel that incorporates the sensation novel in order to resist it, but that nonetheless implies sensation's centrality to the realist project and its appropriateness to any description of modern society.

As in sensation novels, those who exploit knowledge of hidden connections, the possibilities of disguising identities (which, to a certain extent, both Bulstrode and Casaubon do), introduce sensation into the novels. Those who will not be corrupted by the power and money that derives from the past, like Mary and the Garths, like Dorothea, like Ladislaw, escape the sensation plot. Ladislaw's case in this respect is particularly instructive. As the major victim of the plots of Bulstrode and the self-interested passivity of Casaubon, he is on the edge of sensation all the time. He is, moreover, distinctly a foreigner in type and is not a midland man. The crisis of the novel, at least for Dorothea, comes just at the point when she sees evidence that Ladislaw is having an affair with Rosamond – "sensation material" of the first order. But Ladislaw escapes being thrust back into a sensation plot because of his love for Dorothea, and, more important, Dorothea refuses to respond to scandalous possibilities, reads herself out of sensation fiction into realist fiction by refusing to allow herself to be stopped in her moral openness because the evidence is against Will. The moral crisis between Rosamond and Dorothea spins on just this extrication of Ladislaw from the sensation plot, at the same time that Dorothea refuses to believe that Lydgate is in one either. It is precisely the refusal of the general judgment, and the refusal to accept identities thrust upon them (Dorothea, in particular, by the terms of Casaubon's will), that allow Dorothea, Ladislaw with her, to move back into the world of compromise that realism offers them.

The sensation elements are the necessary underbelly of *Middlemarch* as they are of Victorian realism. The reassertion of the "ordinary" against the scandalous and the corrupt is the severe work of the realist mode. But realism depends even for its moral authority on the presence of the corrupt that needs to be investigated and rejected. We see it in Fred's hard work for Mr. Garth; in Mary's quotidian and austere labors; in Mr. Garth's acceptance of the consequences of his loan to Fred. We see it too in Lydgate's scholarly ideal, to which Lydgate aspires and fails: "the exercise of disciplined power – combining and constructing with the clearest eye for probabilities and the fullest obedience to knowledge" (ch. 15, p. 162).

In the light of the usual implications of the sensation novel, one of the ironies of Lydgate's position is that Dorothea's correct assumptions about Ladislaw, but particularly about Lydgate, are utterly unprofessional. All the "evidence" points against Lydgate – in particular, Lydgate's debt to Bulstrode. In a sentence that both implies affirmation of the necessity for the sort of professional investigation the sensation novel sponsored, and of the inadequacy of that, Mr. Farebrother tells Dorothea, "there is no proof in favour of the man outside his own consciousness and assertion" (ch. 72, p. 724). Dorothea stands up for "a man's character," and she makes her determination, not like a sensation novel investigator, but by judging his character and directly asking Lydgate what actually happened. It is clear that her sympathy with the fallen Lydgate reflects as well her disenchantment with the ways the "real world," that is, the world described by the realist novel, constantly compromises ideals: "Oh it is so hard!" she said. "I understand the difficulty there is in your vindicating yourself. And that all this should have come to you who had meant to lead a higher life than the common, and to find out better ways – I cannot bear to rest in this as unchangeable" (ch. 76, p. 752). Lydgate the scientist does have something of the sensation novel "professional" about him. But his profession is not a lawyer-like Robert Audley, or a detective-like figure like Franklin Blake. Lydgate's scientific method is rich with imagination, full of "inward light," and its spaces are "ideally illuminated." As the sensation novel becomes the material that must be in the Victorian realist novel and thrust out of it as well, so realism invites in once more the ideal that the insistent materialism of both sensation and realism attempts over and over again to resist.

V

Money makes the world go around,
the world go around, the world go around,
Money makes the world go around,
it makes the world go round.

The song from *Cabaret*, despite its cynicism, applies precisely to the Victorian novel. There is no more persistent subject and no more significant object. Micawber's lament about how sixpence makes the difference between happiness and suffering, virtually also between life and death, may seem comic and exaggerated. No matter how strongly romantic and moral impulses attempt to repress the fact or belie it, the song pretty much tells the truth of Dickens' work and in different ways of virtually all Victorian novels. The first paragraph of Mary Poovey's anthology on the financial system says almost all:

> As every reader of Victorian literature knows, nineteenth-century Britons were preoccupied with money. They brooded about how to get it, save it, and spend it, and they worried about where money comes from, why it incites so many crimes, and how the well-to-do can live on so little while the poor need so much. The preoccupation was both imaginative and practical. As nineteenth-century novelists and poets turned the national fixation into some of the most engaging fictions of the century, capitalists, bankers, and jurists were forging the financial institutions that enabled money to circulate, international trade to flourish, and Britain to become the richest and most powerful nation in the world.[12]

What the paragraph doesn't say, however, is critically important to Victorian fiction. While money made the Victorian world go round and kept people's heads spinning, it was also extremely difficult to absorb into the moral systems that provided the dominant impulses of their narratives. It is worth reviewing here the argument made earlier, that the Victorian novel seems to be working out in anticipation the thesis of Max Weber in his book *The Protestant Ethic and the "Spirit" of Capitalism* (1905). Simply put, Weber's thesis was that the very qualities of austerity, self-denial, and severe piety that in Europe marked the culture of Protestantism were the virtues that were the most successful in the acquisition of capital.

It was not the money that impelled these Protestant workers to their success, but the work itself, self-abnegating work done for its own sake, for the exercise of self-restraint that the religion urged and required.[13] In the world of *Middlemarch* this curious drama is played out on the screen of a whole community (and implicitly of a whole culture). Like virtually all other mainstream novels, except perhaps for a wonderful aberration like *Wuthering Heights* (where nevertheless money is the instrument of Heathcliff's triumph and power), *Middlemarch* worries repeatedly, with extraordinary variations, about money. Like virtually all other mainstream novels, except perhaps those of Anthony Trollope, it treats the pursuit of wealth and the acquisition of money as marks of corruption. So while, on Poovey's account, virtually all Victorians were passionately concerned with money, virtually no Victorian novelists will treat it as anything but a harsh necessity or a positive evil. Money does seem the root of all evil.

The growth of Protestant forms of piety in Victorian England (leading to the kinds of excesses parodied by Dickens, for example, in *Bleak House*, and Collins in *The Moonstone*, in which the true villain of the piece is a preacher) reflects this double attitude. The enormous social transformations that were producing a solid middle class, defined by its unqualified pursuit of wealth, and displacing the aristocracy, also produced considerable anxiety about the culture's materialism, about the ethical breakdown under a new system of laissez faire, the kind of thing about which Matthew Arnold wrote satirically in *Culture and Anarchy* (1869) when he characterized the emerging middle class with the saying, "I can do what I want with my own." Against this sort of moral coarseness and asocial regardlessness, there was the counter-movement to somehow preserve the values of the religious past in an increasingly bourgeois and secularizing culture.

The Victorian novel, on the whole, was a critical part of this counter-movement. The strong moral vocation that George Eliot took up as a novel-writer is certainly an aspect of the effort, studied sometimes with negative implications in important recent criticism, particularly that of

D. A. Miller, who sees the Victorian novel as a form designed to help shape the rising middle class. And the spirit of that rising middle class had to be infused with the Protestant ethic. A quick review of some of the novels with which this book has been concerned will suggest how pervasive this effort is and how consistently it manifest itself in this strangely self-contradictory stance toward wealth and success. *Vanity Fair* is obviously all about money, and Becky's pursuit of it is the extreme case of corruption, while at the same time Amelia's misery can only be cured by money. *Great Expectations* allows Pip's redemption only after he gives up his "great expectations," and risks all of his inheritance from Magwitch in order to save his life. Jane Eyre inherits money unexpectedly, money that she needs; but she will not keep a pence more than she needs and gives the rest to her cousins. The plot complications of *The Woman in White* are built on the effort to defraud Laura of her money, but when her identity is restored by Hartwright he allows Fosco to keep the money. Here, as in many other novels of far different type, the important thing is, supposedly, not the money but the life (there is no value but life, said John Ruskin). *Lady Audley's Secret* elaborates another plot where identity and money are manipulated. Elizabeth Gaskell's *North and South* attempts to affirm values other than profits, but its plot is only resolved when Margaret inherits (unexpectedly) enough money to allow her to assist her bankrupt lover to restore a humane manufacturing system (which has broken down for lack of money). What is characteristic of all of these novels is that while money is absolutely essential to the plot and to the well-being of the protagonists, no protagonist is shown for an instant as in pursuit of money. Virtue is its own reward, and yet – think back to Richardson's *Pamela* – the reward usually brings with it, unbidden, lots of money.

One of the characteristic Victorian themes – offspring, indeed, of *Pamela* – is the vulnerability of class hierarchies, the social and economic trans-formations that made middle-class merchants more powerful than ancient landed families. In that transition, money could be mistaken for authentic rank, and one of the primary questions with which the Victorian novel dealt was just the question of authenticity, which seemed increasingly separable from questions of wealth. In *Middlemarch* that characteristic plot is only intimated in the relation between Rosamond Vincy and Lydgate. He is of an aristocratic family, though he has abandoned – he believes – their way of life; she is the daughter of a wealthy tradesman and niece of Mrs. Bulstrode, a Vincy married into new money and new power. Rosamond uses her good looks to enter, or try to enter, the aristocratic family of Tertius Lydgate, who, in his turn, attempts to get away from that family to do important work in the world, where money and rank are entirely secondary to talent and knowledge. But the marriage cracks up (or all but cracks up) as a result of inadequate funds. It's as simple as that. Lydgate's aristocratic tastes and "spots of commonness" lead him to live over his head and – in George Eliot there can be no more negative symbol – he is driven even to gambling to try to avoid the bankruptcy that Rosamond can't tolerate.

Money is at the heart of the Bulstrode plot, which also entails questions of identity. His money belongs in fact to Ladislaw, but Ladislaw will have nothing to do with him. The money, in effect, doesn't matter to the good hero, who must make his way in the world by finding a thing to do that is worth doing. Money is at the heart of the Fred Vincy plot. He can only become worthy of Mary Garth if he does not inherit Featherstone's money and finds a thing to do. Mr. Garth, who professes always to be interested only in business, becomes the fullest embodiment of Weber's thesis. For the magical word "business," for Mr. Garth, has absolutely nothing to do with money, but only with work done with the fullest integrity and the most absolute commitment. "I think," says the narrator, "his virtual divinities were good practical schemes, accurate work, and the faithful completion of undertakings: his prince of darkness was a slack workman." But, she adds, "He could not manage finance" (ch. 24, pp. 249–50). In other words, Mr. Garth is the fullest embodiment of the Protestant ethic, and his success at the end of the book is due entirely to the quality of his work and his absolute integrity, which is marked by his refusal of any possibility of gaining money that might be tainted in any way. Money, if it comes, must come unbidden – that is the Protestant ethic, as it is the novelists'.

The Victorians' double attitude toward money creates particular difficulty for the *Bildungsroman*, which, as we have seen, traces the development of parentless young men and women from fantasy to maturity as they come to terms with the realities of their society. They begin with great expectations or great hopes and must learn to make their way in society, and success entails some kind of material comfort. In a newly booming mercantile and industrial economy in which success does indeed mean money and whose ways these novels often unveil, one might expect some material rewards. In most cases, the rewards do come, if more moderately than might have been hoped. But almost none of those material rewards can be viewed as coming from the often nasty workings of so highly competitive a society. Certainly, there are virtually none that are acquired through business (except indirectly) or manufacturing. David Copperfield, for example, wins the rewards not of a businessman but of a successful novelist, and on the way he creates a group that exposes fraudulent practices. Margaret Hale loses her impractical father and gets an unexpected inheritance. Jane Eyre too. Pip gives up his money and works in a minor position in some sort of business, but is not described as having much success within the capitalist world. Penn, too, becomes a novelist. Even in that domestic/epic poem, *Aurora Leigh*, Browning makes Aurora a success as a writer. Maggie Tulliver has no luck whatsoever, and dies. Only in the novels of Trollope can one find upwardly mobile young men who make their successes inside the new economy, and even here, in so many novels, there is little of that.

It is instructive to pause briefly over one example of a novel in which the hero really is described as being one of the central figures in the new economy, that is, Dinah Mulock Craik's *John Halifax, Gentleman* (1856). If there is a novel anywhere that fully exemplifies Weber's thesis, it is this one. For John Halifax is, as Henry James describes him, a pure man. He makes his way up, almost literally from the dung heap, by virtue of his extraordinary virtue. Unlike protagonists in most of the mainstream novels that are conventionally discussed in courses on Victorian fiction, John never makes a mistake, never stumbles morally. His virtues are just those qualities that George Eliot attributes to Caleb Garth, except that he is also good at finances! If he runs into difficulties at any point in his narrative, it is because he loses a beloved daughter, has trouble with another daughter, who is duped by a scheming and worthless aristocrat, and a son who goes temporarily bad. None of the evils is his fault, of course. Reading *John Halifax, Gentleman* is reassuring just because it serves, in contrast, to underline how rich and complex most of the now better-known Victorians are in their treatment of these issues and particularly in their powers of characterization. Nonetheless, Craik's book probably comes closer to the realities of how a young *Bildung* hero might, practically speaking, have achieved success. What is difficult to credit from our distance in time is just the exemplification of Weber's thesis, that one could have come through that formation of character in the world of Victorian business and industry utterly unstained. Or, to push it further, that anyone under any conditions could have come through a difficult life utterly unstained. If mainstream novelists err by ignoring the degree to which the direct pursuit of money was intrinsic to the formation of struggling youth in

Victorian times, Craik errs by suggesting that one can indeed acquire great wealth and remain, as James skeptically put it, "pure."

The nature of the purity, as it is connected with questions of work and class and material prosperity, is clear at the point in the book when John rejects Lord Ravenal's offer of his hand in marriage to John's daughter. The class tables have been turned in this narrative, for here the aristocrat comes to beg of the former child of poverty to be allowed to bring the child into the aristocracy. And John, now rich, powerful, and still austerely pure, will have nothing of it. Of course, Ravenal assumes that his position will win him the girl without question. John is forced by questioning to explain his reasons for rejection. "Would you imply," asks Ravenel, "that anything in my past life, aimless and useless as it may have been, is unworthy of my honor – the honor of our house?" "Aimless and useless" do the work, even for Ravenel, who suddenly recoils, contrasting "with the unsullied dignity of the tradesman's life, the spotless innocence of the tradesman's daughter – what a foul tattered rag, fit to be torn down by an honest gust, was that flaunting emblazonment, the so-called 'honor' of Luxmore."[14] Here is the vengeance of the new middle class against the aristocracy, the overt rejection of class hierarchy. Material conditions are entirely irrelevant to John's thinking – it does not matter that Lord Ravenel is twenty years older than his daughter. It does not matter that Lord Ravenel is from a powerful old aristocratic family. The distance between Ravenel and the Halifaxes is "as wide as the poles," but "Not in worldly things, but in things far deeper – personal things, which strike at the root of love, home – nay honor" (p. 435).

The drama may be external, but the values are all internal. And thus a popular novelist can quite consciously allow John Halifax to become a "Gentleman" because his inner values are never corrupted as they drive him to success in the capitalist world. There is no incompatibility in Craik's novel between the possession of money and the sustaining of honor.

For most of the novelists we have looked at in this book, this is simply not the case. In *Middlemarch* we can watch being played out a series of related dramas in which the key condition, the key act, will be directly connected to the possession (or dispossession) of money, and each one of these acts marks the major moral epoch in these characters' lives.

I will conclude here simply by pointing to several scenes where this moral epoch is achieved. There is Mary Garth, waiting on Peter Featherstone the day he dies, refusing to bring the two different wills to

Featherstone so that he can "change his mind." "Shan't I do as I like at the last," he angrily willfully cries (echoing Arnold's "doing as one likes"). To which Mary replies, "I will not let the close of your life soil the beginning of mine" (ch. 33, p. 313). "Take the money – the notes and gold – look here – take it – you shall have it all." But of course she will not take the money. She "never forgot that vision of a man [acting out the Arnoldian horror of middle-class willfulness and obsession with material power] wanting to do as he liked at the last." The scene becomes an emblem of the moral attitude of the entire book. Narrative after narrative sets personal integrity against money, and only Mary and Caleb can withstand the temptation absolutely, almost in the mode of John Halifax, but less pompously.

Fred's story we have alluded to already. Once the inheritance is lost, he must find a way to make his way in the world, and he turns to Caleb himself, from whom he has ruinously borrowed money already. Mary had earlier said to Fred, "My father would think it a disgrace to me if I accepted a man who got into debt, and would not work" (ch. 15, p. 138). And given that he does work and therefore, as it were, earns Mary, the book rewards him with the Stone Court he had hoped to inherit in the first place. But he gets it without aspiring to it, without corrupting himself in the pursuit of money, as a consequence of learning from Caleb and working hard.

The other stories are more complex, but not less clear. Lydgate, in particular, is a victim of aspiration to material satisfactions, even if he thinks of himself as completely dedicated to his medicine and his research. In all his professional life he is entirely honorable, but Farebrother warns him not to get entangled with Bulstrode. In the end, his debt to Bulstrode and his financial straits implicate him in a shameful, perhaps a criminal act. The one additional point that needs making here is that Dorothea's first advice to him, as the crisis grows, is to return the money to Bulstrode. Which he does. All the characters in the book who are meant to escape, more or less successfully, from moral corruption must at one point or other either refuse money from Bulstrode or turn it back to him. Bulstrode with the power his money gives him is the focal point of corruption, but many are contaminated.

And the romantic drama of the book culminates in Casaubon's will, which denies Dorothea inheritance from him if she marries Ladislaw. Of course, it is a cowardly and even disgusting thing to do, but the book needs it as it works out the problem of how to emerge morally from the mess of interconnections, social and economic, that the novel dramatizes. When she is told of the codicil in his will saying that "the property was all to go away from you if you married . . ." she replies "impetuously," "That is of no consequence" (ch. 50, p. 482). Money does not matter, but the book cannot stop talking about it.

In the light of the problems money causes to the moral clarity of Victorian fiction, it is striking that the intensely romantic scene in which Dorothea and Ladislaw first kiss is marked by considerable talk about money and wealth. Just before the kiss, Ladislaw says to Dorothea: "I shall most likely always be very poor: on a sober calculation, one can count on nothing but a creeping lot" (ch. 83, p. 796). It is a characteristic Victorian moment in which the man in effect gives up his true love because he will be poor and he cannot ask her to marry his poverty (or, in marrying, to allow him her wealth). He returns to the subject again after the kiss, even when Dorothea gives some encouragement: "It is a mere toss-up whether I shall ever do more than keep myself decently, unless I choose to sell myself as a mere pen and mouthpiece" (p. 797). Even here, money is envisioned as corrupting. To stay honorable is to stay poor. At the critical moment, after exclaiming, "My heart will break,"[15] she movingly formulates the vision that dominates the Victorian novelists' attitude toward money: "I don't mind about poverty – I hate my wealth" (p. 798).

The irony and the difficulty of this attitude is that the novelist knows that money is indispensable anyway. Dorothea does give up Casaubon's money; she does move to London, where Ladislaw seems to make some kind of honorable success as a politician (although of course we are not given access to the details of that part of Dorothea's life). Moreover, Dorothea is not left penniless without Casaubon's money anyway. The money is there, but for the Victorian novel, this part of the story is better left untold. Money focuses the moral crises of Victorian fiction and of its effort to come to terms with the culture transforming all around it.

VI

In *Middlemarch* virtually all the qualities of realism described in chapter three are in play. The *Bildung* narratives so deeply embedded in it are precisely the narratives of Victorian realism – the minute attention to particulars of time and place, the dailiness of domestic life, and more broadly, of the small community, the carefully researched historical background to the story, the disillusionment that follows as the quotidian displaces the ideal, the compromises that material and psychological reality impose on the ideal and that, in the end, make life possible, the reiterated sense that the trivial is rife with significance and that everything is connected. These are marks of Victorian realism, intensified by the sophistication of George Eliot's technical mastery and powers of psychological observation as she constructs and comments, exploring the possibility of knowing and making the very medium of language visible to careful readers.

In returning to the subject of realism here, however, the point will be to look at some of the ways in which George Eliot, convinced as ever that epistemology and ethics are one, presses the techniques almost to the breaking point, and makes it hard not to recognize their potential contradictions. Moral realism is not so confined to the ordinary as it pretends; it is not so confident about its capacity to represent the real as its name suggests; it is not so clear about what is real as its tries to be; it is not capable, aesthetically or morally, of escaping the pressure of the ideal on its imagination of the way things are.

It is not only that "sensation" lies just beneath the surface of the everyday and ordinary that is the ostensible subject of realist narratives. The very representation of the "real" world of nineteenth-century England threatens to belie the enormous and often conflicting energies of the emerging new social and economic orders. The conflation of aesthetic, epistemological, and moral commitments in a literary form – the novel – whose responsibility it was to entertain and educate and somehow improve the largely new reading public, was inevitably incomplete, riven with conflicts. Realist fiction, designed as a kind of celebration of the ordinary, of the new bourgeois moral order, of the potential sacredness of the commonplace, needed finally the ordinary's other face – its insecurity about class, money, and identity, the hidden desires, the inevitable incompleteness of its work.

Reality in *Middlemarch* is a complex tangle of connections, a society in motion, identities in flux, a whispering chamber, a constantly shifting set of relations, a roar on the other side of silence. No Victorian novel carries further the commitment to set its narrative tightly in history, to set its characters tightly in society, to see the object as in itself it really is. But *Middlemarch* is also so tremblingly sensitive to the reality of interconnections and to the limits of every thing in itself as it encounters other things in themselves and defines itself by such relations that, in the end, it threatens to crack the very technique of realism to pieces.

The *ideal* frames the entire narrative and hovers over its working. Notoriously, *Middlemarch* begins with the ideal – a figure that contrasts with the complex, compromised condition of the modern real – St. Theresa. And thus, although the story of St. Theresa is precisely the kind with which Victorian realism will not deal, it is also the story that it tries to tell over and over. The "Prelude" is in part an announcement of what is not possible in the modern world (the world of the novel itself) and in part an affirmation of the realist technique of implying the presence of the ideal in the ordinary. In effect, simply by its presence, it tells the whole of the story: modernity allows no "epic life," and realism is the technique that disallows such a narrative. And yet, the compromised, mistake-filled world that it describes is the offshoot of "a certain spiritual grandeur" ("Prelude," p. 3). It is an easy move from St. Theresa to the austere and naïve "Miss Brooke," whose name makes the first words of the first chapter, but that transition implies a history, an entrance into modernity, a falling away from spiritual grandeur into something, as George Eliot implies, even harder – a life of spiritual striving that has "no sacred poet" to describe it and that sinks into "oblivion." Behind these words is the imagination of the realist novelist who will sit in for the "sacred poet." The "Prelude," in other words, raises the stakes of the realist novel, by implying, as the narrative sinks back into the materiality of modernity, that the material resonates with the ideal.

The "Finale," without re-evoking St. Theresa, dissolves Dorothea into the multiplicities and dailiness of modern life, and back into the ideal as well. In the narrator, Dorothea has, after all, had her "sacred poet," but that poet can record not the "epic life," but a "full nature" that "spent itself in channels that had no great name on earth." The narrator invokes "the growing good of the world," pressing her largely deflationary narrative, full of losses and compromises, to the service of some larger good, achievable in some date distantly beyond the end of the novel, to be achieved by gradual, incremental change. That is, she imagines the world somewhat the way Darwin did: the world changes not as the result of great catastrophes and sudden revolutionary transformations, but from small, slow changes accumulating through time. George Eliot as realist was in this sense a uniformitarian – what happens now is the same kind of thing as happened then. Mountains are not developed overnight, but through millennia of earthquakes that raise the earth a few inches at a time; species do not change overnight, but over more than millennia, one characteristic minutely transforming from generation to generation to generation until finally the difference from the original is so great that its character has completely diverged from its origins. The responsibility of the realist, then, is to record the unhistoric. The "sacred poet" is the author of the new bible of the realist novel, the home of unhistoric acts.

The presence of the ideal in the material is dramatized immediately after the "Prelude," in the very first chapter, serio-comic in style. Dorothea, against the demands of her own self-imposed austerity, responds with visceral intensity to the gleam of light on the jewels she intended to renounce. "How very beautiful these gems are!" The intensity of the response emphasizes the dramatic irony, particularly as Dorothea's unexpected enthusiasm is perceived by her sister, Celia, who wants those gems too. Entirely sensible, Celia is annoyed at her sister's inconsistency, pleased, however, to recognize that Dorothea might not be so perfect after all, as she tries "to justify her delight in the colours by merging them in her mystic religious joy" (ch. 1, pp. 13–14).

Dorothea's incoherence, and her desperate attempt to connect two ostensibly disparate parts of herself, makes her vulnerable to Celia's commonsense criticism. The play of points of view and the brilliance of the description make that little, unlikely scene a remarkable projection of the two young women's characters and suggest much of their stories in the book to follow. It is the unveiling of this unselfconscious arrogance as a reflex of a genuine generosity of spirit that gives the chapter a satirical edge (and keeps Dorothea from being the goody two shoes, the angel in the house, so often criticized by anti-Victorians). But it also brings immediately to the forefront a fundamental contradiction in Victorian fiction. The scene can be taken as a kind of parable. As Dorothea cannot reconcile her visceral attraction to worldly beauty with her deep piety, so the realist novel has trouble reconciling its commitment to representing a literal, material, historically shaped present with the ideal energies that often drive it.

In Lydgate, though in a very different way, the ideal and the material play against each other. In a passage to which we have had occasion to allude several times already, Lydgate values the "imagination" that

Reveals subtle actions inaccessible by any sort of lens, but tracked in that outer darkness through long pathways of necessary sequence by the inward light which is the last refinement of Energy, capable of bathing even the ethereal atoms in its ideally illuminated space. He for his part had tossed away all cheap inventions where ignorance finds itself able and at ease: he was enamoured of that arduous invention which is the very eye of research, provisionally framing its object and correcting it to more and more exactness of relation; he wanted to pierce the obscurity of those minute processes which prepare human misery and joy, those invisible thoroughfares which are the first lurking-places of anguish, mania, and crime, that delicate poise and transition which determine the growth of happy or unhappy consciousness. (ch. 15, p. 163)

The scientist's project as Lydgate imagines it is surely the realist's project. The material reveals itself fully only to the imaginative, to the idealist. The narrator, like Lydgate, has done away with "all cheap inventions" (or at least has tried to do that), and has labored rigorously, capturing the details of provincial life and the facts of history in that period roughly forty years before she began writing. But just as the "Prelude" and "Finale" show her unhappy with the bleak news that realistic representation has tended to bring her – the failures and compromises that are the condition of life in the here and now – so she shows herself to be unhappy here with the idea that realism (or science) is merely a method of representation, a passive subjection to the way things are. Rather, she dramatizes through Lydgate's consciousness the idea that adequate representation, realist representation, requires "imagination," requires "arduous invention."

Through such rigorous labor at registering the material and working with "the last refinement of Energy," that is, "inward light," Lydgate and George Eliot bring together the workings of human consciousness and imagination; the material and the ideal are brought together. Her realist project is just Lydgate's scientific one, to locate in consciousness itself, in its material and spiritual elements, the very sources of human misery and joy. It is at this point that George Eliot's realism, refined to minute psychological precision throughout *Middlemarch*, begins to look like something other than realism, requiring another sort of language and method in which the connections and crossings that mark reality in the Victorian novel are quite literal – based in the minute processes of mind. (While this is a literal representation of developments in physiological psychology among the Victorians, it also seems to anticipate our contemporary efforts to map the brain and account for traits of human behavior encoded in our DNA and in the physical structure of the brain.) With such minute and intricate investigation and crossings over between imagination and mere reporting, Victorian realism begins to move away from the apparently simple grounds of the ordinary, the domestic, the material in the world of consciousnesses, such as Henry James would come to focus on, and a world of imaginative freedom from the constraints of the material and the historical.

Objects are usually important to any realist project, and they are to George Eliot as well. Objects clearly described add that touch of verisimilitude to realistic texts that makes the characters' lives more plausible and comprehensible, even if those objects play nothing but their normal quotidian roles. In George Eliot, however, objects are not nearly as important as they are in a Dickens novel or even a Thackeray novel. Their worlds are sometimes almost defined by the plethora of things, sometimes rich with significance, like the Johnson's dictionary given to Becky when she leaves the training academy and which she throws out the window of the coach; some function as part of a larger condition that establishes a quality of character or a social context; some few are just there, part of the pleasure of the text.[16] Realism, however, almost always has to come to terms with the necessity to make the real representative (an almost paradoxical project). Objects need to "mean" as well as just be.

In George Eliot, objects, the clothing people wear, the food they eat, the furniture they choose, while carefully realistic, virtually always push toward meaning, almost as in allegory – although of course realism asserts itself against that most artificial of literary forms. George Eliot rarely tells her readers much about what her characters eat (as against a world of food and drink in Dickens, on any page of whose works one is likely to find more references to food, drink, pieces of furniture, dinner ware, than George Eliot is likely to offer in whole chapters). In *Middlemarch*, she throws the action inside, and registers objects as part of the panorama of mind and consciousness. Of course, it matters a great deal what furniture Lydgate buys and what he has to sell off to keep himself afloat financially, or what sort of horse Fred rides, or what sort of clothing Dorothea and Rosamond wear. George Eliot is alert to things as any realist must be, but they are likely to be bearing a heavy burden of meaning. In this respect, she is a realist like other Victorians, yet her thrust toward meaning is, on the whole, more consistently intense.

The difference – and it is only in degree, not in kind – is that in *Middlemarch* in particular, objects almost always carry with them a weight of meaning that readers ignore at their peril, but which readers accustomed to Victorian novels would not miss. Beginning with those jewels, so brilliantly registered both objectively and through the minds of the two sisters, there is much narrative and psychological work being done. The emerald and diamonds that for a moment overwhelm Dorothea with their physical beauty do their work of forcing the reader to recognize what Dorothea tries to rationalize away, the reality of her body and of physical desire. Mr. Casaubon's mole, which so disgusts Celia, is irrelevant to Dorothea, but tells Celia and us that Casaubon is both unattractive and a disaster for a sexually vital young woman like Dorothea.

The intensity of George Eliot's moral realist work leaves her world thick with meaning, and in that way moves realism toward its antithesis, allegory. Of course, *Middlemarch* remains firmly realist, but the intensity of meaning that it radiates with every description turns the real world into a vast sounding space of signification that fellow Victorian realists tend not to achieve with such thoroughness, or do not even attempt to achieve. It is another aspect of *Middlemarch* that moves it to the very edge of realist possibility because, in particular after the publication of Darwin's *Origin of Species* (1859), the natural world threatened to be drained of any meaning beyond itself. Meaning in that world can only emerge, not from the material world out there but from human consciousness. George Eliot may indeed often take the stance of the omniscient narrator, looking down on her subjects with scientific detachment. But her "objectivity," if that is what we want to call it, is often exerted by finding ways to register the consciousness of her characters, and the material world enters those consciousnesses not "objectively" at all, but shaped by desire, distortions of perspective, personal and bodily limits. And since nobody in the novels is outside that material world, with interests and desires at work, it becomes clear in *Middlemarch* that the narrator herself can see only within the limits of her own interests and desires. The idea of realist rendering of the world with no sense of mediation is strongly undercut by the novel. Every object is alive with meaning. "Signs," as the narrator says, "are small measurable things, but interpretations are illimitable" (ch. 3, p. 25).

Barbara Hardy has pointed out how moments of revelation and disenchantment in George Eliot frequently are expressed in terms of landscape,[17] and a supreme example of this use of the material world as the expression of a state of mind and feeling comes in chapter 28, when Dorothea returns from her wedding journey asking herself, "What shall I do?" (p. 271). The narrator is strongly attentive to physical appearances there, as Dorothea emerges from her toilette with the "healthful glow" of youth, with the "gem-like brightness on her coiled hair and in her hazel eyes," and the "warm life in her red lips." But what she sees is "the low arch of dun vapour," the "stifling oppression of that gentlewoman's world." "Her blooming full-pulsed youth stood there in a moral imprisonment which made itself one with the chill, colourless, narrowed landscape, with the shrunken furniture, the never-read books, and the ghostly stag in a pale fantastic world that seemed to be vanishing from the daylight." The key phrase here is "made itself one." For in perhaps less direct ways, the landscapes and objects of *Middlemarch* turn themselves into attitudes, feelings, ideas, and do the work of internal analysis even as they assert themselves as objective description.

It is worth mentioning at least one other of many elements in *Middlemarch*, oddly common, in its unrealistic way, to much Victorian realist fiction. Casaubon's estate is, certainly not accidentally, called "Lowick," a perfectly Dickensian name in its suggestion of his absence of vital energy. "Middlemarch" is certainly allegorically loaded in its insistent middleness, not only literally to indicate the English midlands, but metaphorically to connote the middling, ordinary life that realism takes as its subject. Other names in the book are not so obviously charged with significance, but each one echoes with hints: Casaubon the medieval scholar. Garth, an old English name that gives us "yard" or "garden" and fairly suggests Mr. Garth's calling and his upright old-fashionedness. It is not clear exactly what "Bulstrode" signifies, perhaps something of the coarseness and aggressiveness that marks him off from Middlemarch neighbors, but it is perfectly suggestive in a Dickensian way, like "Podsnap," for example, or "Bagstock." The names have no distinct literal meaning that might apply to the character, but suggest just what kind of character someone so named would be. This kind of character typing, a holdover from older not quite realist literary tradition, is certainly not George Eliot's dominant mode, but it is a common practice of even the most realistic of novelists, and here it is part of a thoroughgoing effort to load the world with meaning, to make realism extend beyond its literal descriptive limits. Realism always threatens to descend into the kind of meaningless and endless sequence of events, things, and perspectives that Biffin, in *New Grub Street*, was trying to capture. George Eliot resisted that turn of realism, as did most of her contemporaries. In the face of a world from which a designing God had been removed,[18] George Eliot imagined one that retained its meaningfulness through the messy, sloppy, and myriad details of ordinary life. Biffin's realism, on her accounting, could not tell the full story. This banal and ordinary world is shaped with moral meaning.

The issue of "meaning" raised in this consideration of the realism of *Middlemarch* opens out what is often taken as the most interesting and innovative aspect of the book, the one that takes the issues of interpretation, knowability, perspective, and multiplicity of signification and makes of them a dominant theme and a self-reflexive one. It is in this respect that *Middlemarch* most obviously pushes Victorian moral realism to its limits. Elaine Freedgood has tried to show that despite appearances, George Eliot is entirely committed to standardizing meaning and attempts to instruct her readers, with their powers of imposing illimitable meanings on things, on how to get at the right meaning.[19] But it may be yet more fruitful to regard *Middlemarch* as a battleground in which George Eliot's attempt to generate the "right" meaning out of a world of other possibilities is countered by her own relentlessly truthful representation of the possibility of other meanings. The implication of herself as narrator among those inside the story whose interpretations are always partial and incomplete threatens the very basis of Victorian realism. As should have been clear, especially in the discussion of Thackeray, this problem was neither new nor unique to Victorian realism. The difference in *Middlemarch* is only George Eliot's theoretical insistence on the problem, an insistence that makes of *Middlemarch* a kind of culmination of the Victorians' most serious questioning of the realism the vast majority of Victorian novelists practiced.

There are many passages in *Middlemarch* that force readers to reflect on the very practice of realist representation. If the object of realist fiction is somehow to gain access to the thing as in itself it really is, then the comment about the illimitability of interpretation threatens the possibilities of success. And this is particularly true if the idea that the narrator herself is "interpreting" gets jarred loose from its applications to the characters in the novel and hangs over the entire narration. One of the most famous lines in Victorian literature opens chapter 29: "One morning, some weeks after her arrival at Lowick – but why always Dorothea?" The first part of the sentence lulls readers into feeling that the story is proceeding normally; the second part shakes them into attention to the fact that the story isn't just happening, but is being narrated, and that narrator and readers are in silent and unacknowledged agreement about the way narration will happen, about what counts and what doesn't, about each other's trustworthiness. The interrupted sentence dramatizes the fact that this agreement is merely conventional, that there is nothing inevitable about the way the story develops, and that – here of course is George Eliot's major point – there are ethical consequences to these apparent innocent conventions.

The broken sentence implicates the narrator as much as it does the readers. She too has been seduced, both by the quiet way in which any narrative does not announce what it is not describing and thus does not announce the choices it is making with every word, and by the attractiveness and interest of her heroine. If you write about one person, you can't be writing about the other person. Minimally, one recognizes that even the least attractive of figures, like Casaubon, has "an intense consciousness within" and is "spiritually a-hungered like the rest of us" (ch. 28, p. 275).

It is a legitimate criticism of this move by George Eliot that, in the end, despite some exploration of that consciousness, the weight of the novel comes down heavily on Dorothea's side, and as for Casaubon – well, good riddance to bad rubbish. Despite several brilliant pages of free indirect discourse in which the reader is invited to explore Casaubon's pathetic mind and spirit, it is clear that the narrator is not dispassionate at all: "For my part," she intrudes, "I am very sorry for him" and for that "small hungry shivering self" (ch. 28, p. 277). Skeptics about George Eliot's sympathy certainly have strong grounds in the treatment of Casaubon.

Nevertheless, it is important to recognize the way George Eliot's shift of focus reminds readers not only of Casaubon's equivalent center of self but of the reality, unmarked directly in the novel, of a whole world of people with which the book is not concerned. That is, as George Eliot attends to the partiality of any representation, her technique reminds the reader (even in a preachy tone occasionally) of their own narrow perspective. If we should be paying attention to Casaubon, shouldn't we be paying attention to other people with which the book is not concerned at all? Of course, it is the narrator's narrow perspective as well. Earlier on, in an almost equally famous passage, the narrator explains her method, looking back to an age when there was more genius and more time, but indicating that she is impelled to do other work:

> I at least have so much to do in unraveling certain human lots, and seeing how they were woven and interwoven, that all the light I can command must be concentrated on this particular web, and not dispersed over that tempting range of relevancies called the universe. (ch. 14, p. 130)

The realist has to choose her subject, narrow it, and avoid the tempting range of relevancies. But given the commitments of the book and the passage itself, it isn't as though all the other things in the world not attended to are irrelevant. Just as the human lots she traces are "woven and interwoven," so in fact there is no place in the universe to stop, since everything is connected to everything else. The realist novel is deliberately, necessarily, arbitrary. Some limiting principle, a principle that will falsify reality even as it makes recording it possible at all, has to be imposed if there is to be a book at all. Every perspective is limited and every narration is inevitably prejudiced, even discriminatory.

The moral implications of this apparently obvious point about the necessity of limits haunts the book, however, and haunts the realist project, and most obviously in another of the book's most famous passages. It is both a passionate call to realism and an announcement of its impossibility (at least at the moment):

> That element of tragedy which lies in the very fact of frequency, has not yet wrought itself into the coarse emotion of mankind, and perhaps our frames would hardly bear much of it. If we had a keen vision and feeling of all ordinary human life, it would be like hearing the grass grow and the squirrel's heart beat, and we should die of that roar which lies on the other side of silence. As it is, the quickest of us walkabout well wadded with stupidity. (p. 192)

The roar that lies on the other side of silence includes not only Mr. Casaubon's equivalent center of self but the whole world that lies beyond the very few human lots with which the novel is concerned or with which any human being can engage. In this passage, George Eliot intimates a reality that realism can only intimate. And perhaps the very immensity of that reality justifies the artist's decision to focus attention on a small cluster of characters, but at the same time demand a recognition of the absolutely limited moral and epistemological vision this narrowing entails.

Encountering these irresolvable difficulties, *Middlemarch* tries, in good Victorian compromised ways, to engage the knowable and the ethically doable as best it can. But the roar that it intimates makes, even for the few individual human lots, the comic ending that had marked Victorian realism through most of its history almost impossible to sustain. The Victorian novel continued to struggle toward some satisfying vision of a world increasingly complex, increasingly crowded, increasingly hard to decipher, increasingly secular, and increasingly driven by social and economic forces that were unequivocally self-interested. Dorothea may contribute to the growing good of the world, but that "good," as one might seek it in later fiction, looks increasingly problematic – Isabel Archer, Milly Theale, Tess of the D'Urbervilles, Jude the Obscure, Lord Jim, all wait over the horizon of the Victorian novel to face something much closer to tragedy than even Dorothea was to know. One way to think of the modernist novel's rejection of Victorian realism is as a final recognition of the impossibility and the terrible pain of the project, and the overwhelming power of that roar on the other side of silence. A commitment to art as containing, limiting, designing, is also a commitment to find means to incorporate that roar without dying from it.

Notes

1   For a discussion of this subgenre, see Peter Garrett, *The Victorian Multiplot Novel* (New Haven: Yale University Press, 1980).
2   The importance of empire to the Victorian novel has been the subject of much recent criticism, much of which has focused on how the empire lies, unrecognized, in the various business concerns of novel characters – as in *Dombey and Son*, or in secrets that underlie the money and power of the newly empowered classes, as in *The Moonstone*, or even in Thackeray's *Vanity Fair*. Although I do believe that a full study of the cultural implications of the Victorian novel would have to include an extensive section (as Edward Said tries to provide in his *Culture and Imperialism*), the indirectness of the empire's presence in Victorian fiction until the last twenty years of the nineteenth century makes emphasis on it in a book like this more dutiful than useful. For an interesting introductory discussion of the presence of empire and race in Victorian fiction, see Nicholas Dames, " 'The sun and the moon were made to give them light': Empire in the Victorian Novel," in Francis O'Gorman, ed., *The Victorian Novel* (Oxford: Blackwell, 2005), pp. 4–24.
3   Jerome Beaty, "History as Indirection: The Era of Reform in 'Middlemarch,'" *Victorian Studies*, 1 (1957), pp. 172–9. Beaty shows with what care George Eliot introduces news about the events in London leading up to the passage of Reform at critical moments in the novel.
4   *Middlemarch* (Oxford: Oxford University Press, 1996).
5   Rosemarie Bodenheimer, *The Real Life of Mary Ann Evans, George Eliot* (Ithaca: Cornell University Press, 1994), p. 174.
6   For a detailed discussion of the ways parts publication affected the novel, see Jerome Beaty, *"Middlemarch" from Notebook to Novel* (Urbana: University of Illinois Press, 1960), particularly pp. 44–55. This volume is the fullest and best treatment of the making of *Middlemarch*. While Beaty's book is one of the most valuable scholarly contributions to the study of George Eliot, it does not at all press the possibility that other than aesthetic considerations influenced any part of its writing.

7   The romance is a form that minimizes historical and material restraint on character to release the character to be fully responsible for her own choices and thus her own fate. Henry James exploits this mode in *Portrait of a Lady* (1881), a novel partly influenced by *Middlemarch*. It gives more freedom and thus makes the protagonist fully responsible for her own moral choices. George Eliot is too committed to realist context to develop this mode thoroughly, but Dorothea's story is much closer to the romance ideal than, for example, is Lydgate's.

8   Rosemary Ashton, *George Eliot: A Life* (London: Penguin Books, 1996), p. 286.

9   Gillian Beer, in "George Eliot and the Novel of Ideas," in John Richetti, ed., *The Columbia History of the Novel* (New York: Columbia University Press, 1994), p. 455, argues that chance, improbability, and the sorts of scenes that these things bring into the novel are not merely "a ruse of the novelist but a reminder of the multivalency of the world, visible when attention is fully aroused." While I do think that this is right, Beer's analysis, emphasizing the complexity of George Eliot's vision, does not quite sufficiently emphasize the importance and the difficulty of these scenes that violate not only the "rules" of plotting in realist fiction, but violate the decorum of realism, its focus on the ordinary and the quotidian. That is to say that the multivalency of the world Beer rightly notes includes just those elements that are the staple of sensation fiction.

10 The one important critical study that recognizes fully the importance of sensation plot elements for the work of Victorian fiction and of realism is Alexander Welsh, *George Eliot and Blackmail* (Cambridge, MA: Harvard University Press, 1985). Welsh shows that some of the same functions that I have described the *Bildungsroman* as serving are served by sensation elements. He talks particularly of blackmail, but that of course entails all kinds of dirty secrets, including murder, crime of all sorts, illegitimate sexual relations, and so on. He argues that *Lady Audley's Secret* is "a representative Victorian story of blackmail . . . in the implicit threat to membership in a social class, in the mobility that makes secrets of social origin possible, and in the transformation of justice into a routine of concealment and exposure" (p. 22).

11 Several important critics, most particularly D. A. Miller and Alexander Welsh, have pointed to the Foucauldian argument that the nineteenth century is an age of surveillance. Welsh seems to me right in arguing that this is not always bad news, but Miller's discussion of the policing implicit in Victorian fiction picks up an important aspect of the work of "sensation" within the mainstream novel.

12 Mary Poovey, *The Financial System in Nineteenth-Century Britain* (Oxford: Oxford University Press, 2003), p. 1.

13 See Max Weber, *The Protestant Ethic and the 'Spirit' of Capitalism* (New York: Penguin Books, 2002). Weber argues: "So if an inner affinity between the old Protestant spirit and modern capitalist culture is to be found, we must try, for good or ill, to seek it *not* in its more or less materialistic or at least antiascetic enjoyment of life (as it is called), but rather in its purely religious features" (p. 7).

14 Dinah Craik Mulock, *John Halifax, Gentleman* (New York: W. M. H. Allison, nd; 1856), ch. 36, p. 436.

15 The outcry echoes the outcry of Lucy Snowe in *Villette* when she is about to lose M. Paul to his family. When a heroine cries out like that in a Victorian novel, she has reached the snapping point at which mere conventions, which keep women suppressed, are found to be so intolerable that rebellion bursts from their hearts. In George Eliot, and most particularly in Brontë, the moment is a powerful one in particular because Lucy Snow is not only repressed by conditions, but has trained herself never to let her feelings be observed by others.

16 For a very useful discussion of the way objects work in a culture of consumption, see Andrew Miller, *Novels Behind Glass* (Cambridge: Cambridge University Press, 1995).

17 See Barbara Hardy, *The Novels of George Eliot* (London: Athlone Press, 1959). "The disenchanted day-lit room is one of her most important recurring scenes of crisis" (p. 190).

18 George Eliot fell away from Christianity some years before, and in 1846 translated David Strauss's *Leben Jesu*, which analyzed the language of the Bible to recover the real historical Jesus. While she ceased believing in Christianity (she was to translate Feuerbach's *Essence of Christianity* in 1854), she believed in the ethical vision of the world that Christianity had projected, and this vision, both materialist and ethical, is infused in her realistic fiction.

19 Elaine Freedgood, *The Ideas in Things* (Chicago: University of Chicago Press, 2006). Freedgood understands that this is a very contentious argument, and, in discussion of *Middlemarch*, usefully summarizes the alternative position. She also offers an extensive interpretation of the jewel scene, concluding that "Dorothea's true heirloom . . . is her plain dress" (p. 131). In Freedgood's interesting analysis, objects are indeed loaded with meaning, but the novel resists alternatives and attempts to control their meaning from within George Eliot's range of values. The question remains whether that meaning is represented in a way that keeps it stable or that opens it up into the multiple ambivalences of modernism.

Index